Don't open this compelling book before the cook calls "Supper's ready!" You won't want to put it down, even to eat. Alice (Aliki) Padova Anderson has shared a lifetime of flavors and fun; for forty years she's been "commuting" between Columbia, Mo., U.S.A., and her native Corfu, one of the hundreds of islands along the coast of Greece. Special artistic treatment of the author's photographs adds an interesting dimension to the more than 240 pages of unique recipes and interesting family stories.

Alice makes it easy for us mainlanders to create dishes which call for ingredients not available in the "states." She often suggests substitutes and has adjusted some recipes to appeal more to an American palate. We may not actually need to know to gather snails after a rain when they're crawling on the trunks of trees and how to keep them from crawling out of the container as you take them home. It's important to know that it takes more than an hour to "cook an octopus till tender" – (information that makes one appear intelligent in after-supper chit-chat).

You'll find out why Alice, age 12, vowed never again to carry a live turkey on a bicycle. You'll learn to make coffee "that sings to you" and how to vary the recipes for fish, squash, zucchini, and other foods that can pile up in the kitchen in season. The generous use of herbs, spices, onions and garlic makes the recipes mouth-watering – just to read them.

You'll be proud to own Alice Padova Anderson's "CORFU COOKING, Recipes and Stories From a Greek Island," dedicated to her Mother, Maria Argyropoulou, who encouraged her to explore the world of cooking.

- Columnist and author, Sue Gerard

Corfu Cooking

FAMILY RECIPES AND STORIES FROM THE GREEK ISLAND OF CORFU

by

Alice Padova Anderson

Illustrations by John Pyle

Published by
Athena Publishing Company
P.O. Box 584
Columbia, MO 65205

Dust jacket design by John Pyle
Graphic design by Jan Wiese-Fales, Fertile Mind Designs

Printed in Jefferson City, Missouri by Modern Litho-Print Co.
Manufactured in the United States of America

International Standard Book Number: 0-9727971-0-6
Library of Congress Control Number: 2003101683

In essence, this cookbook
is a tribute to my mother,
Maria Argyropoulou,
who encouraged me to explore
the world of cooking.

❦

ACKNOWLEDGEMENTS

My thanks to Sandy Roberts for typing part of the manuscript.

❦

I am indebted to Nina Johnson for her invaluable contribution in many ways. First I thank her for her interest in Greek food and Greek culture. Her computer skills and talent as a librarian helped me to manage the many recipes, stories and other pieces of information. She brought the manuscript together. Nina has been patient, supportive and has opened new avenues for my endeavors.

❦

My appreciation goes to my illustrator, John Pyle, and to my graphic designer, Jan Wiese-Fales, who were able to grasp the cultural nuances of my country.

❦

A word for Bill Claasen, my tough and merciless editor, who helped me to become a better writer.

❦

To all my friends who ten years ago insisted that I write a cookbook, thanks. This is my gift to you.

TABLE OF CONTENTS

Recipes

Stories

INTRODUCTION

I was born and raised on the island of Corfu, Greece, where I spent the first twenty years of my life.

Even as a child I enjoyed cooking, learning early on to cook by feel, taste and smell. From an early catering experience as an adult, I discovered how much I also enjoy sharing my culture through cooking and that was a primary motivation for writing this book.

My other motivation was the discovery of four little red notebooks containing all of my mother's recipes – recipes for the foods that I grew up with, prepared by those I loved most. Mother's notebooks contain her own recipes and those of her friends and family. I feel strongly about preserving both my own cooking and food heritage, as well as that of my mother and her contemporaries. Some of the recipes are unique and to my knowledge are not found in any other Greek cookbook.

Corfiot cooking has many influences, including a strong influence by the West. For a long time the seven Ionian islands were separate from Greece, to be united with Greece in 1864. Venetians, French and English have passed through Corfu as conquerors or protectors. Many dishes have an Italian name or a name of Italian origin (for example, Fish Bianco, Pasta Frolla and others). The English left their mark with puddings and a few dishes have a Turkish influence, brought by Greeks who escaped from the mainland. Corfu has distinct foods and food dishes that I will summarize in the Corfiot Cooking section that follows.

Most of the recipes in this cookbook are my mother's. A few are indigenous to Corfu. Others are traditional Greek recipes and still others are my own.

Throughout the book I have included personal stories about my family and our neighborhood on the island of Corfu; stories directly or indirectly related to the growing and gathering of food, its preparation and the enjoyment of eating and sharing it.

Alice Padova Anderson

CORFIOT COOKING

Bourtheto - Bourtheto comes from the Italian "brodetto," a fish stew. Brodo in Italian means broth or soup. Bourtheto and brodetto are both fish stews with a few differences, bourtheto being the hotter of the two.

The fish is cooked in tomato sauce, onions, garlic and a lot of red pepper. The favorite fish for this recipe is scorpios, a bony fish; however, other types of fish can be used.

Bianco - (Italian term for white). Bianco is a fish recipe. Usually whiting or gray mullet is used. Fresh Mediterranean cod can be used as well as dry salted cod. The fish is cooked in its own broth with oil, lemon juice, garlic and sliced potatoes. The potatoes absorb the flavor of the fish that is used. This is one of the island's typical dishes.

Cod Fish Pie - This pie, not made with phyllo, is traditionally eaten the last Sunday of Carnival just before Lent begins.

Corfiot Olives - These olives are black, tiny and sweet. They are used to accompany appetizers and entrees. They are not used in the production of virgin oil.

Pastitsada - The best pastitsada is made with chicken. However, other meats can be used. I have even seen a recipe using lobster. The meat is cooked in tomato sauce with onions, cinnamon and cloves. It is served with spaghetti, macaroni or other types of pasta which is mixed with the thick sauce.

Poulenta - (English term is polenta) - A porridge made from corn meal boiled in water. Tomato sauce can also be added. With the addition of raisins, nuts, and milk, it can become a dessert.

Savoro - Fried fish, usually sardines, preserved in a sauce of rosemary, vinegar, garlic and raisins.

Tsigareli - Wild greens cooked with oil, garlic, tomato sauce and red pepper or paprika.

DESSERTS AND FRUITS

Mandolato, mandoles and kumquats, or cumquats, are Corfu specialties.

Mandolato - This nougat is made from glucose, honey, sugar, meringue, rosewater and browned almonds. It is sliced into bars and served.

Kumquat or cumquat - A small citrus fruit imported by the English from the Japanese in the mid-19th century. The fruit is used to make preserves, candied fruit and liqueur.

Strawberry Ice Cream - Corfu is also famous for the quality of its ice cream, especially the one that is made from local strawberries. They are aromatic and small.

Fogatsa - A type of sweet bread prepared for Easter.

Loukoumades - Honey puffs traditionally made on Saint Spyridion Eve, which is celebrated on December 12. Saint Spyridion is the Greek Orthodox protector of Corfu. Loukoumades are prepared throughout the winter months.

Pandespani - A type of sponge cake.

Pasta Frolla - A type of shortbread covered with apricot preserves.

Tzaletia - A mixture of cornmeal and raisins spooned and fried in olive oil and sprinkled with sugar. It is good for breakfast or dessert.

Pavlosika (Frangosika) - Also known as a prickly pear, it is a sweet, aromatic and tasty fruit very popular in Corfu. It is usually eaten cold. The skin has thorns that have to be removed prior to peeling the fruit.

Sikomaida (Sikopita) - Made from sun-dried figs which are cut into pieces and seasoned with anise seed, pepper and ouzo. This mixture is wrapped in fig leaves and left to dry.

Tzintzoles or tzitzifa (jujubes) - A small red fruit with a pit. It can be eaten fresh. It can also be baked in the oven, then pitted and seasoned with ouzo and anise seeds. It is oftentimes served as a dessert to accompany wine.

Tsitsibira - A drink characteristic of the Greek Ionian Islands. It was introduced into the islands by the British. Tsitsibira is prepared with lemon juice, ginger root, water and sugar. It is then fermented for a period of time.

Tasty creams and rizogala (rice puddings) are found in special shops specializing in dairy products.

Appetizers

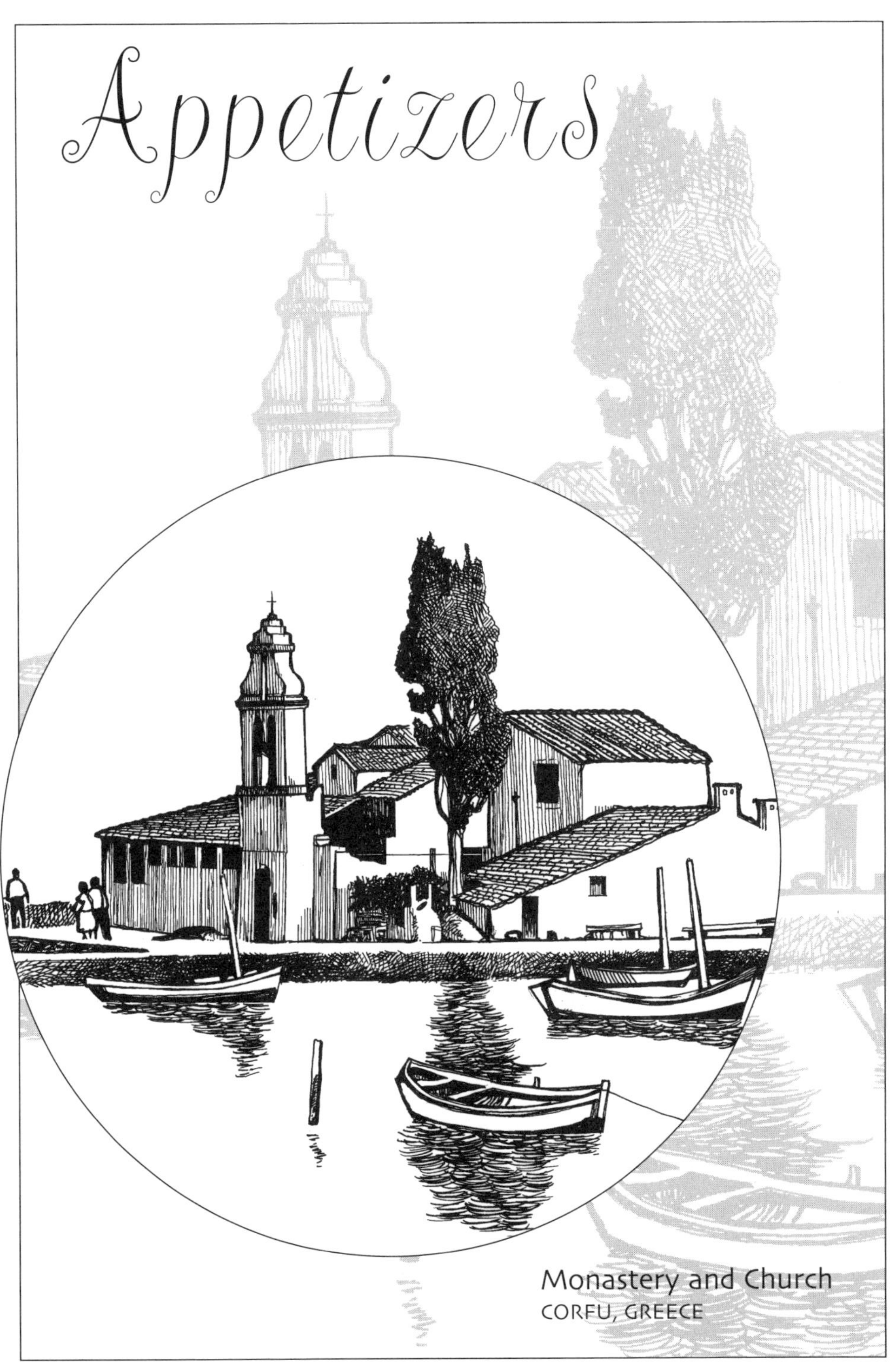

Monastery and Church
CORFU, GREECE

APPETIZERS

Appetizers, called mezedakia, are very popular in Greece. Their variety is inexhaustible. Accompanied with ouzo or wine, they can be eaten separately or as part of a meal.

Tavernas, restaurants, and ouzeri offer a great array of appetizers each using their own imagination to create tasty and succulent morsels of food. Mezedakia can be eaten hot or cold.

A whole meal can be planned using a variety of mezedakia. Some can be served as a first course such as dolmades or meatballs. Others can be prepared in larger portions (cheese or spinach triangles) and become a main course.

If you are planning a buffet with appetizers, I would suggest a couple of dips such as tzatziki and eggplant dip, and a couple of salads such as fish roe, eggplant salad and village salad. To these dishes, add dolmades, small meatballs, a few pies, olives, feta cheese and sliced hard-boiled eggs. For fish dishes, include fried kalamari, or octopus, in oil or vinegar. Sliced peta bread and crisp rolls can accompany the food choices.

For a more complete buffet, add a selection of the following: roasted leg of lamb, pastitsio and moussaka. Complete the selection with desserts such as galatoboureko, revani, nut cake and baklava. Reserve cakes for tea time.

BOUREKAKIA

Makes 50

Bourek, a Turkish word, means "bite-size appetizers." Usually it refers to a variety of small appetizers filled with cheese, meat, poultry or fish mixtures. Tyropetakia is an example of a bourek. It is wrapped in commercial or homemade phyllo and fried or baked and should be made fresh and served hot. Cheese, spinach and chicken pie recipes can be used to make small appetizers. Other ingredients can also be substituted. Experiment with the pie recipes included in the section which begins on page 59.

1 pound of hamburger
2 tablespoons tomato sauce
1/4 to 1/2 cup oil
1 small onion or 4 fresh green onions chopped
2-3 sprigs of parsley chopped (discard the stems)
1/2 cup of water
Salt, pepper, garlic salt to taste
3 eggs lightly beaten
10 tablespoons of Parmesan cheese or Greek Kefalotyri cheese

Simmer the ingredients, except for the eggs and cheese, until all the liquid is absorbed. Let cool. Add the eggs and grated cheese.

Dough

5 cups flour

1/4 cup oil
Juice of 1 lemon
1 teaspoon baking soda
Salted water

Pour flour into a bowl. Add oil and mix well. Add soda and lemon juice. Add enough salted water to make a stiff dough. Roll out a pastry sheet thicker than phyllo. Cut circles 3 1/2 inches in diameter with a glass or cutter. Fill with one teaspoon of the mixture. Fold in the middle and secure the ends by pressing them together. Fry in a pan of hot oil until golden brown on both sides. Serve hot.

Instead of frying, you can bake the bourekakia in a 350° oven for 20-30 minutes until golden brown. Serve hot.

FRIED SQUID (KALAMARI)

2 pounds squid
Juice of 2 lemons
Salt and pepper to taste
Flour
Oil for frying

Wash squid. Place in a strainer to drain.

Cut squid into 1 - 2-inch pieces. Flour the squid and fry in hot oil. When the pieces become light brown, place in a serving dish and pour lemon juice over them. Serve hot.

CHEESE TRIANGLES (TYROPETAKIA)

Makes 40-50 pieces

8 - 12 ounces feta cheese
6 ounces cottage cheese
3 eggs
1/2 cup chopped parsley or dill
1 pound phyllo pastry
Melted butter

Crumble feta cheese into small pieces. Add cottage cheese with slightly beaten eggs and blend thoroughly. Mix in the parsley or dill. Layer as many phyllo sheets as you are going to use. Cut phyllo sheets into five-inch strips.

Put a teaspoon of the filling one inch from the end nearest to you. Fold the phyllo in order to form the triangles. Seal the last triangle with a little water.

Place triangles in a well-greased baking sheet. Brush them lightly with butter. Bake approximately 45 minutes at 350° until crisp and golden. Serve hot.

Although feta cheese is the most commonly used cheese, Kasseri or Kefalotyri (hard cheese similar to Parmesan) can be used. Soft ricotta, cottage cheese, Mizithra, or mozzarella can be used with feta cheese for a milder taste. Use your imagina-

tion and combine the cheeses you like to suit your taste.

FREEZING: Tyropetakia can be prepared in advance and frozen, baked or unbaked.

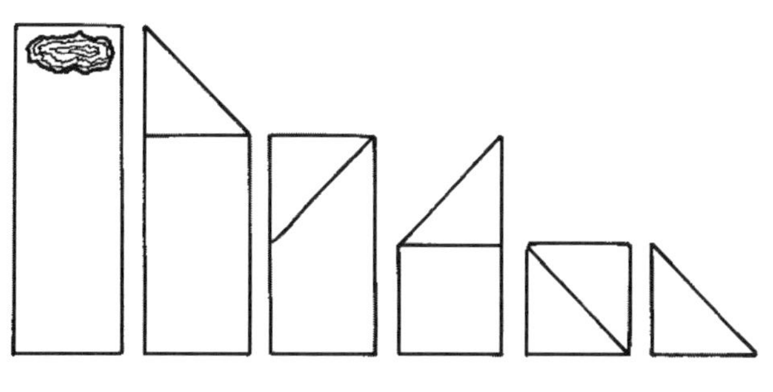

POTATO CAKES

Makes 20-25 patties

2 pounds potatoes

2 eggs

4 tablespoons Parmesan cheese

4 tablespoons minced parsley

Fennel or dill

Oil for frying

Salt and pepper to taste

Flour

Boil potatoes. Cool. Peel and puree. Add all the other ingredients and mix well. Form into small patties two inches or more round. Roll in flour and fry until golden brown. Serve hot.

VARIATION: You can substitute the Parmesan cheese with crumbled feta cheese.

DIP WITH YOGURT (TZATZIKI)

1 cup plain yogurt drained
1 small cucumber peeled and shredded
4 - 6 cloves of garlic thinly sliced
1 - 2 tablespoons oil
Salt or garlic salt to taste

Drain the yogurt with cheesecloth if needed. Peel and shred cucumber. Put it in a bowl. Add salt which will help drain the liquid. Drain and squeeze the excess liquid. Add the yogurt, oil, garlic and seasoning and stir.

Eat tzatziki as a dip with grain breads or peta.

EGGPLANT DIP WITH YOGURT

1 cup peeled eggplant pieces boiled and drained
3 tablespoons parsley
1 small pepper diced
4 tablespoons yogurt
4 tablespoons oil
Juice of 1 lemon
Breadcrumbs to thicken
Salt and pepper to taste

Place the ingredients in a blender and mix until you get a dip consistency. Add breadcrumbs to thicken the mixture to your taste. Pour in a serving bowl. Garnish with olives and/or wedges of tomatoes.

EGGPLANT DIP WITH MAYONNAISE

1 medium eggplant
2-4 tablespoons mayonnaise
2-4 tablespoons olive oil
Juice of 1 lemon
Basil minced
Breadcrumbs to absorb liquid if needed
Salt and pepper to taste

Place eggplant on a baking sheet. Make a few incisions so that the steam can be released. Bake for 40 minutes at 475° until eggplant is soft. Scoop the inside out and discard excess seeds. Put it in a blender and puree. Transfer to bowl and blend in small amounts of mayonnaise, oil, lemon juice and basil. Season as you go along until the flavor is right for you. You may or may not use the total amount of mayonnaise and oil suggested.

CHICKPEA DIP WITH TAHINI

1 15-ounce can of chickpeas drained and rinsed
2-3 tablespoons tahini
2 cloves garlic sliced
4 tablespoons water
Juice of medium lemon
2-4 tablespoons of olive oil
Salt and pepper to taste
1 tablespoon minced parsley (optional)
Parsley and/or olives for decoration

Mix all ingredients in a blender. Begin with the chickpeas, garlic and water. Add the rest of the ingredients and blend. If too thick, add more water or oil.

OCTOPUS WITH VINEGAR

Cook octopus in seawater or salted water for 30 minutes or until it is tender. Remove from water. Cut in pieces. Transfer to a bowl. Cover with half vinegar and half water. Let it stand in the liquid for 4-5 days in the refrigerator. Remove from liquid and serve as an appetizer with oil, lemon juice and black pepper.

You can find octopus in some food stores and fish markets.

OCTOPUS WITH TOMATO SAUCE

2-3 pounds octopus
1/2 - 1 cup oil
2 tablespoons tomato paste
8 ounces tomato sauce
2 medium onions cut into pieces

Cook octopus in seawater or salted water for 30 minutes or until it is tender. Cut into pieces.

Dissolve tomato paste in some water. Put all ingredients and enough water to cover octopus in a pan. Cook on medium heat until it is done.

Serve the sauce with macaroni or spaghetti.

OCTOPUS WITH OIL AND GARLIC

2-3 pounds octopus
1/2 - 1 cup oil
5-6 cloves of garlic, minced
Oregano
Salt and pepper to taste

Cook octopus in seawater and/or salted water for 30 minutes until it is tender. Drain and cut in pieces. Put in skillet, add the oil and the minced garlic and cook until it is done. Once the octopus is cooked, add the oregano.

CHICKPEA PATTIES

Makes 10 patties

15-ounce can of chickpeas
1/2 onion minced
1 egg
2 tablespoons parsley
Salt and pepper to taste
1 teaspoon oregano
2 tablespoons Parmesan cheese
Flour for rolling
Oil for frying

Drain and rinse chickpeas. Blend in a blender or food processor until smooth. Sauté onions in oil until tender. Mix all ingredients and shape into small patties. Roll in flour and fry in hot oil. Serve them hot.

ZUCCHINI PATTIES

Makes 12-15 patties

2 cups grated zucchini
1/2 onion minced or grated
8 ounces feta cheese
2 tablespoons parsley
3/4 cup flour
Oil for frying
Salt and pepper to taste

Grate zucchini and squeeze out the liquid. Mix all ingredients to form a dough. Form patties or spoon the mixture into hot oil and fry. Serve hot.

STUFFED GRAPE LEAVES (DOLMADES)

Makes 6 servings

Dolmades are stuffed with a combination of rice and ground meat or plain rice and served during Lent. I am giving you the recipe with the rice mixture, referred to as Dolmades Yalanzi, which is a vegetarian dish.

1 jar grape leaves (8 ounces)
1 cup rice
1/2 - 3/4 cup oil depending on your taste
Juice of 1-2 lemons depending on your taste
2 medium onions chopped fine
2 tablespoons tomato paste
1/4 cup parsley chopped fine (mint or dill or a combination of both can be used)
Salt and pepper to taste
1 teaspoon ground coriander or cinnamon (optional)
Water

Wash grape leaves under cold running water to eliminate the brine. Remove the thick stems. Soak rice in water for 30 minutes. Drain. Sauté onions in part of the oil for a few minutes. Add some water and cook until tender. Add rice, tomato paste and seasoning. Cook for five minutes while stirring occasionally. Add lemon juice and parsley and continue

cooking until liquid is absorbed.

Spread out each leaf and place one teaspoon of the filling in the center. Starting from the stem, roll up the leaf while tucking in the sides until you have a tight little package. Place the dolmades close together in a saucepan. To avoid scorching, line the saucepan with a few grape leaves. Pour in enough water to barely cover them. Add the remaining oil and lemon juice. Place a heavy plate over the dolmades to prevent them from unrolling. Bring the liquid to a boil. Lower the heat and cook for about one hour until rice is tender. If the water is absorbed, you may add more water. Serve warm or cold. Accompany with yogurt or tzatziki.

VARIATION: You may add a couple of tablespoons of raisins or pine nuts to the mixture.

A popular Greek appetizer, dolmades go very well with a Greek anise aperitif called ouzo.

SPINACH PIE TRIANGLES

Makes 50-70 pieces

3 ten-ounce packages chopped spinach
2 medium onions finely chopped
8 ounces feta cheese
8 ounces mozzarella
5 eggs
1/4 cup oil
Fresh dill or mint
1 pound phyllo pastry
Butter

Thaw spinach and remove all moisture. Sauté onions for 5 minutes in oil. Add the feta, mozzarella, dill and slightly beaten eggs to the spinach. Stir until well-blended. If too watery, add some bread crumbs.

Use the method described under cheese triangles on page 14 to assemble the spinach triangles.

Place triangles on a well-greased baking sheet. Brush the outside with butter. Bake at 350° until crisp and golden.

If you don't need this quantity, you can freeze half of the triangles to thaw and bake at a later date.

Soups

Pontikonisi (Mouse) Island
and Monastery
CORFU, GREECE

SOUPS

Greek soups are thick and substantial. They are the main dish, particularly Fasoulatha (bean soup). It is considered a staple to be eaten with bread, a piece of cheese and a piece of onion. Soups have nourished generations of Greeks, especially in the villages. Bean, lentil or garbanzo soups are very popular during winter time because they are hot and nutritious. They also provide the opportunity for the cook to demonstrate her skill at combining ingredients.

I have never eaten two bean soups that taste the same. And I was never able to duplicate my mother's bean soup with the ingredients that were available in the United States.

In my family's household, two days a week were designated as soup days. Actually we called them spoon days. Our spoon days were Wednesday and Friday. I loved some soups and I hated others. I loved my mother's bean soup which was thick and creamy. I have included this soup recipe in the book. I must admit that with the use of convenience foods, soups in Greece have taken a secondary role.

Greeks also use chicken, meat and fish broths for soups. Meat or fish is usually served as a separate dish. Avgolemono soups can be made from any of these broths and vegetable soups are made with summer or winter vegetables.

BEAN SOUP (FASOULATHA)

Makes 6-8 servings

1 pound dried beans (white Northern)
2 carrots sliced
2 stalks celery sliced
1/2 pound spinach or Swiss chard chopped
2 small onions or leeks, chopped
1 cup chopped fresh tomatoes or 1 can diced tomatoes
Tomato sauce to taste
1/2 cup oil
Salt and pepper to taste
1 bay leaf
Two sprigs of parsley

Soak beans overnight. Drain and dispose of water. Put the drained beans in a pan and cover with water. Boil until tender, 2-3 hours, depending on the beans. I process beans in a pressure cooker and cook the vegetables in a separate pan. When the beans and vegetables are tender, I combine them. Then, I add the oil, tomatoes, tomato sauce, bay leaf and let them simmer over a low heat for at least one hour. Another way of doing it is to add the uncooked vegetables the last hour you cook the beans.

A variety of canned beans can be used.

This is a very popular soup. Thick and tasty, it can be served as a main dish. We eat it with bread, feta or kasseri cheese, olives or smoked herring.

The Aunts (Les Tantes)

Like three peas in a pod, Tante Helen, Tante Bellina and Tante Chariclea were the same height and the same size but they had very different dispositions. Tante Bellina was sweet, Tante Helen was domineering and Tante Chariclea was the mediator between the other two. Because my aunts were elderly and single, they developed certain characteristics of their status in life. They were extremely inquisitive and very talented at uncovering detailed information about their neighbors. But they didn't simply discover and accumulate information. They would then broadcast the information throughout the neighborhood. My immediate family became the target of their investigations. The tantes, who were really distant relatives, lived in the house across the street from our house. They were always on the alert for every knock on our door or any movement in our yard. Strategically seated behind the window, they would pull back the window curtain slightly, observe and then quickly disappear behind the veil of lace. We knew they were there but we could not prove it.

"They were extremely inquisitive and very talented at uncovering detailed information about their neighbors."

I was frequently the victim of their curiosity. If I entered our yard carrying a package or a bag, the sisters would open the window and ask me what was in it. Innocently, I would respond by giving them every detail of the contents. I would also freely offer the details of my family's everyday life.

I was a frequent guest at their table, not because they were good cooks but because they needed more information and as you might imagine, the elderly private investigators would frequently invite me to dine with them. They sought out stories and descriptions.

I recall complaining to my mother that the tantes' soups were too thin, their potatoes uncooked and their almond balls rancid. I remember the blue ceramic bowl containing the almond balls, coming out of the cupboard for the first time. I counted the sweets. There were nine. Over the months, almost a year, there were three balls remaining in the bowl. By that time, the almond balls had changed color and taste. The sugar coating had fallen away and collected at the bottom of the bowl.

Because I never told them how much I disliked their almond balls, they would always offer me another one. And because mother had instructed me to be polite, I always accepted what the three sisters offered to me. So, I would dutifully eat the rancid sweets, conscious of how many were left in the bowl.

VEGETABLE SOUP

Makes 4-6 servings

3 medium potatoes diced
2-3 medium carrots chopped
2 stalks celery chopped
2 medium zucchini diced
2 medium onions chopped
2 medium tomatoes diced
1/2 cup oil
Salt and pepper to taste
Beef stock or chicken stock

Sauté the onions in the oil and then add the stock and vegetables. Boil on medium heat for 1 hour.

Try for taste. Add lemon juice on your individual plate and sprinkle with Parmesan cheese.

You can make your own combination of vegetables. Add a leek, spinach, cabbage or other vegetables to your liking.

CHICKPEA (GARBANZO) SOUP

Makes 4-6 servings

1 pound dried chickpeas

2 onions diced

1/2 cup oil

Salt and pepper to taste

Rosemary leaves

Fresh lemon juice

Soak chickpeas overnight. The next day, drain and dispose of water. Put the chickpeas in a pressure cooker. Cover them with water and cook until tender. Discard the skins if you don't like them. Dispose of the water. Add water to cover the chickpeas. Add the onions, oil and rosemary leaves. Cook until the water is absorbed and the soup is thickened.

The chickpeas can be cooked on top of the stove. Put the drained chickpeas in a pan. Cover with water and bring to a boil, then add the onions and rosemary leaves. Reduce heat and simmer for about two hours until tender. Add the oil at the beginning of the simmering.

Serve with fresh lemon juice.

The onions and lemon juice tend to thicken the soup. In order to soften the chickpeas and shorten the cooking time, many cooks use soda in the soaking water. Soda was never used in my family. Canned chickpeas can be used to reduce the preparation and cooking time.

PASTA SOUP WITH TOMATO SAUCE (PASTA KOLOPIMPIRI)

Makes 4 servings

This soup is made in Corfu. It is often prepared very hot. I make it less hot by using mild pepper and/or mild paprika.

1 cup pasta (kritharaki or orzo) uncooked
1 onion minced
3 cups of water
2-4 tablespoons tomato sauce
Oil for sautéing
Salt
Black and red pepper to your taste

Sauté onion in oil. Add tomato sauce and cook to the consistency of a sauce. Add seasoning. Pour in 3 cups of water and bring to a boil. Add pasta and cook until done. Add some water if needed.

The soup should be thick and peppery.

Some cooks add seasonal vegetables.

CAULIFLOWER SOUP

Makes 4 servings

1 pound cauliflower florets
1 pound potatoes peeled and sliced
1 medium onion sliced

1 cup milk
2 tablespoons oil
Juice of 1 large lemon
Salt
Nutmeg to sprinkle on top (optional)

Place sliced potatoes, cauliflower and onion in a saucepan and cover with water. Let them cook until soft and half the liquid is absorbed. Process vegetables with the liquid in a blender. Return to pan. Add the milk and 2 tablespoons of oil. Cook for a few minutes. Add the lemon juice and salt. Salt according to personal taste. Salt has the tendency to bring out the lemon taste.

CRACKED WHEAT (KOFTOS) SOUP

Makes 3-4 servings

1 cup cracked wheat
3 cups water
2 tablespoons oil
Salt and pepper to taste

Cook the cracked wheat in the water for 10 minutes. Lower the heat and cook for another 10 minutes until the cracked wheat is soft but crisp. Add the oil at the end of cooking.

To garnish, serve with crumbled feta cheese and parsley. For a thinner soup, add more water.

POTATO SOUP

Makes 4 servings

2 large potatoes (2 pounds)
1 medium onion sliced
1 cup milk
2 tablespoons oil
Juice of 1 lemon
Salt and pepper to taste
Nutmeg (optional)

Cook potatoes and onions together in enough water to cover them. Cool. Mix the vegetables and water in the blender and pour back into the pan. Add the milk, salt, and pepper, and bring to a boil. Before serving, add the lemon juice and oil and mix for a few minutes. Remove from burner and serve. Sprinkle with nutmeg.

To bring the soup to a desired consistency, you may want to add more milk or water.

Kritharaki is a very popular Greek pasta that means barley. It is shaped like a long-grain rice but thicker in the middle. It resembles the Italian orzo which also means barley.

GREEK PASTA (KRITHARAKI) SOUP

Makes 4 servings

3 cups water
1 cup kritharaki
1/2 onion thinly sliced
4 tablespoons tomato paste

1/4 cup water

2 tablespoons oil

In a pot, pour the water in with the onion. Dilute tomato paste in the 1/4 cup water, add to the onion and bring to a boil. When it starts boiling, add the pasta and the oil. Cook for 10 minutes, stirring occasionally with a wooden spoon. Lower the heat and cook for 10-15 more minutes until soup is thick. For a thinner soup, add more water. Serve it with crumbled feta or Parmesan cheese.

EGG-LEMON CHICKEN SOUP WITH BARLEY

Makes 4-6 servings

6 cups chicken stock

1 carrot sliced

1 stalk celery sliced

1/2 cup broccoli chopped

1/2 cup barley

Egg-lemon sauce (Avgolemono)

2 eggs

Juice of 2 lemons

Combine first 5 ingredients and cook until vegetables are tender. Follow the directions for Egg-Lemon (Avgolemono) Soup on pages 38 and 39.

Tante Bellina

Tante Bellina was the prettiest of my aunts, not because her name suggested it but because she was simply a pretty lady. She was also mild-mannered and very kind.

Bellina had neither the sharp tongue of Tante Helen nor the intellect of Tante Chariclea. She was not as curious and inquisitive as the others. Bellina was a follower. Because of her passive character, she was often blamed for things she did not do. And, she was always the last one to peek out the window if her sisters gave her the opportunity.

Tante Bellina visited our house frequently. She was able to slip in and out of our lives almost without being noticed. Hunger was the reason for Bellina's frequent visits.

During the war, my aunts had few resources. They depended upon their brother who lived abroad and who was not able to send money to them on a regular basis. After his death, the sisters had to cut down on food expenses. Their house went unpainted and repairs were postponed. When Tante Bellina came to our home, Mother would always give her food to take back with her; a potato, a head of cabbage, greens from our garden or eggs from our hens.

Tante Bellina liked me. She would frequently talk and play with me. I would take a book to my aunt and she would read to me. Mother discouraged the book reading because she did not want Bellina in the house for long periods of time. Mother thought, and rightfully so, that my aunt would take the opportunity to snoop around our house and report back to Tante Helen at the command post. "The General," as we sometimes called Helen, would then initiate visits to our house based on Bellina's intelligence reports. Based on the reports from Bellina, Helen would ask invasive questions and make outlandish demands. One day I played a little game with Tante Bellina that I later regretted. As usual, Tante Bellina followed me around the house, noticing everything in sight. Our potato crop had just been harvested from the garden and stored in a large bucket under the kitchen counter. "Come and see," I said to Bellina. "Look how big they are. Here, have one." "Thank you," she responded, as she fondled the large potato in her hands, probably thinking of her next meal. "Do you want another one?" I asked. "Oh yes, that would be lovely." So, I gave her another one and another and yet another. She bent her arms at the elbows in order to make room for all of the potatoes. I was taking nasty pleasure in witnessing her struggling with the potatoes. And, I gave her even more. When my aunt dropped some on the floor, we both kneeled on all fours trying to recover them. For me, it was fun. But Tante Bellina was overwhelmed. So much food was a godsend to her. I was on my hands and knees retrieving the tenth potato when I heard Mother's voice behind me.

> "Hunger was the reason for Bellina's frequent visits."

"That's enough. You can take them home, Bellina. They will make a nice meal for all of you," said Mother. When Bellina departed Mother kneeled beside me. "It was very nice of you to give Tante Bellina the potatoes," Mother told me. "We want to share but we don't have so many. From now on you can give her two, only two. Do you understand?" Mother was caught between feeding my aunts and feeding her own family and trying not to discourage my desire to share. She was kind enough to support the three sisters whenever she could.

There are certain events in my life that have remained imprinted on my mind for years. Forty or fifty years later, Mother talked about an incident with Tante Bellina that upset her. I was involved but I remembered few of the details. However, Mother described it to me so vividly that I was able to recreate the situation.

In the afternoons, Mother would feed me a custard made out of milk, corn flour and sugar. It was a common food for babies and small children. Grandmother would cook the custard, pour it into a bowl and my mother would feed it to me.

One day, when Mother was feeding me custard, there was a knock on the door. It was Tante Bellina. When my aunt came into the kitchen, I settled into my chair and obediently opened my mouth every time a full spoon of custard was directed my way.

After the usual greetings, Tante Bellina stood in one corner of the room watching the feeding. She observed each step of the process and recreated it as if she was the one that was being fed. Her lips would part and her mouth would open slowly in anticipation of the sweet delight. When the spoon disappeared into my mouth, Bellina would close her mouth and her eyes, imagining the sweet custard in her own mouth. When she swallowed there was a look of satisfaction and serenity on her face. Then she would open her eyes again and follow the process with the next spoonful of custard. Bellina would not look at me but she would never let the spoon out of her sight. The scene was repeated over and over again.

EGG-LEMON SOUP (AVGOLEMONO)

Makes 6-8 servings

Generally the soup is made from chicken stock but fish stock can be substituted. Even stock from a few chicken bones is acceptable. It is a light, nourishing soup and very tasty. But the taste is acquired.

8 cups of chicken stock
1/2 cup of rice
3 eggs
Juice of 2 lemons
Salt to taste

Bring the stock to a boil. Add the rice. Reduce heat and cover. Cook the rice until it is tender but not mushy, 12-15 minutes. Add the salt.

Remove from heat but keep warm.

To prepare the avgolemono: In a bowl, beat the eggs for 1-2 minutes until frothy. Add the lemon juice and continue beating. Take a ladleful of the hot stock and add it slowly to the egg-lemon mixture while beating continuously. Add another ladleful slowly, beating the mixture or stirring it with a wooden spoon. Transfer most of the stock to the egg-lemon mixture, equalizing the temperature to avoid curdling of the eggs. If it curdles, you are left with egg-drop soup which is not Greek.

After transferring most of the stock into the bowl, pour it back into the pan and place on a very low heat until the soup thickens, stirring it constantly. I know it is ready when it is velvety, when it coats a spoon and the sides of the casserole. I determine the amount of salt and lemon by taste. In the last stage of cooking, I taste the soup often. I find that a little more salt brings out the lemon taste more distinctly. So I add a little extra salt until the taste is to my liking. If the soup is not thick enough for your taste, add one tablespoon of flour, or one teaspoon of corn starch diluted in water.

Avgolemono soup can be a meal in itself. Adding more rice will make it very thick. I have eaten soups that were so thick they had a pilaf consistency.

Pasta can be used instead of rice. I use the Greek kritharaki which is shaped like rice. Orzo is another pasta that can also be used.

Egg-lemon soup is one of the most popular soups in Greece. In Greek, avgo means egg and lemoni means lemon.

I find that making avgolemono takes patience, skill and hard work but it is worth it.

Tzia Kerkyra

Tzia* Kerkyra, my mother's aunt, lived with us from her early nineties until her death. She was Grandfather's older sister. He loved her very much.

Tall, with a bent-over humpback and slouching shoulders, she was very active in the garden and in the house. She cooked, cleaned and laundered.

Tzia Kerkyra was soft-spoken and very much aware of her secondary position in the household. She was unmarried and under the supervision of my grandmother.

Standing at four feet, three inches tall, my grandmother was a commanding lady not to be ignored. She would say, "I am the mistress of this household and you do as I say." Grandmother would not give an inch and she would mercilessly criticize anyone opposing her views. Being very diplomatic, Tzia Kerkyra would always ask for Grandmother's opinions and seek her approval for certain activities in the household. Tzia Kerkyra was a very intelligent and enterprising lady. She raised hens in an enclosed area of the garden and sold their eggs year-round in the neighborhood. To placate Grandmother's authority and intolerance, Tzia Kerkyra would share a few eggs with her. That kept the peace between them. Although Grandmother had frequent fits of jealousy toward my aunt, Grandfather never attempted to reconcile their differences. He would say, "Let the women resolve their differences." He finally quit escorting them to public places because he didn't want to deal with their bickering.

"Being very diplomatic, Tzia Kerkyra would always ask for Grandmother's opinions and seek her approval for certain activities in the household."

Tzia Kerkyra knew how to cook and cook well. Grandmother never acquired that talent, although she greatly enjoyed eating what was prepared.

Our garden produced many varieties of squash and gourds. Tzia Kerkyra would prepare an excellent squash soup that Mother and I did not prepare for years afterwards because it reminded us of World War II and the occupation. Unfortunately, we never wrote down that soup recipe, but I can always remember its smooth texture and pleasant taste. I have recreated this soup and provided two variations of the recipe.

ஐ

** Tzia is the Italian word for aunt. Barbas is a common word for uncle. In my generation we tended to give those names to the elderly relatives or acquaintances. These words were used as a title because our relationship with these people was not always one of aunt or uncle.*

SQUASH SOUP WITH PAPRIKA

Makes 4-6 servings

1 big potato cut into pieces
2 cups yellow squash grated
3 cups water
1/2 onion diced
2 cloves garlic minced
2 tablespoons parsley minced
Salt and pepper to taste
2 tablespoons paprika
2-3 tablespoons oil

Sauté onion and garlic in the oil.

Add water and potato pieces. Let them boil for ten minutes.

Add squash, parsley, salt, pepper and paprika. Let it cook until it thickens. Add water if needed.

When it cools, blend in a blender.

SQUASH SOUP WITH TOMATO SAUCE

Makes 4-6 servings

1 big potato cut into pieces
2 cups yellow squash grated
3 cups water or stock
4 tablespoons tomato sauce
1/2 onion diced
2-3 tablespoons oil
2 tablespoons chopped parsley
Salt and pepper to taste
1 tablespoon oregano

Sauté onion in the oil.

Add water and potato pieces. Let them boil for ten minutes.

Add squash, tomato sauce, parsley, salt and pepper. Add oregano last.

Add more water if needed.

When it cools blend in a blender.

Try this soup with butternut squash. Add cinnamon and cloves for seasoning. You can also try it with zucchini squash.

I remember the soup being very smooth. I assume that Tzia Kerkyra passed it through a food mill. There were no blenders at that time.

LENTIL SOUP

Makes 4-6 servings

1 pound lentils
1 onion finely chopped
8 garlic cloves chopped
2 bay leaves
1/2 cup oil
1/4 cup vinegar
1 8-oz. can tomato sauce (optional)
Salt and pepper to taste

Wash lentils and put them in a pan with enough water (4 or more cups) to cover them. Boil 5-10 minutes. Add the onion, garlic, bay leaf, oil, vinegar and salt. Cover with additional water and boil until tender. If you are going to use tomato sauce, add to the other ingredients.

If you prefer more vinegar or oil, add it to your individual plate when served. Garlic cloves can be chopped or boiled with the skin. When boiled you can easily eat the tender part and discard the skin.

TOMATO SOUP

Makes 4-6 servings

2 pounds tomatoes (4 medium)
1 medium onion minced
3 stalks of celery chopped
3 cups water
2 scallions or green onions chopped
2-4 tablespoons oil
Salt and pepper to taste

Cut the vegetables into pieces.

Peel and cook tomatoes for 10 minutes. Add onion and celery. Cook until tender but not mushy. Put in blender and blend. Return to pan. Add the water and the chopped scallions or green onions uncooked. They give flavor to the soup. Add 2-4 tablespoons oil and seasoning and let it cook until thick.

Serve with Parmesan cheese on top.

Depending on the season, tomatoes can be more juicy than usual. You might have to adjust the amount of water according to the juice. Start with 2 cups of water and add more as needed. If tomatoes are too acidic, add a pinch of sugar.

Other in-season vegetables can be added in small amounts.

When tomatoes are in season, this is a hearty soup to make. Yet, it is light for the summer. Preferably serve it cold.

Ririka

In my family's large garden, we raised sheep for milk, meat and wool. Our mattresses and pillows were stuffed with their wool and our rugs were made from their skins. We even processed some of their wool into fine yarn that was used to knit sweaters, scarves and socks for Greek soldiers during World War II. We always had three or four ewes and one ram. During the spring, the ewes had their babies and father supervised and assisted with their deliveries. He knew approximately when they would deliver. He would keep them in the barn and visit them in the middle of the night to check on them.

> "Her first year she gave birth to one lamb. But, the second year, she birthed triplets. Riri, Rika and Rikos, the male."

As I grew older, Father started taking me with him to witness the births. I even helped in one delivery. I was there primarily to keep the ewe quiet.

"My little midwife helper," Father would proudly say to me.

I remember when our ewe, Tita, was delivering for the first time. When her labor had prolonged for many hours, Father became concerned. Tita obviously needed help. We entered the stable. I held Tita and talked to her while father inserted his slender hand into her. First, he found the lamb's right leg and gently pulled it out. Next, he found the left leg and pulled it out. Then he disengaged the cord from around the infant's neck and slowly brought out the head.

"All three have to come out together," he told me. When the head and legs were out, Father held onto the lamb's neck and pulled it out together with the legs. In no time, the little body fell onto the hay and Tita gave a sigh of relief. Soon we heard a bleating. The lamb was alive and well.

"Let Tita clean him," Father advised. "She has to accept him." And Tita did just that.

Ririka was our beloved ewe. Her first year she gave birth to one lamb. But, the second year, she birthed triplets. Riri, Rika and Rikos, the male. Rikos never fully developed but his long hair gave him the appearance of a well-fed, healthy animal. We gave him to a neighbor who wanted him for breeding purposes. The neighbor was impressed by his long hair. Father never saw any of Rikos' offspring.

We expected Ririka to produce two to three lambs the following year. But that never happened. She became ill and we knew that she would die. Mother, the practical one in our family, said, "Let's slaughter her." Father and I refused to hear such a suggestion and we replied emphatically, "No!" We wanted her to die with dignity. We gave her a funeral service and we buried her under a lemon tree where she frequently lay to protect herself from the afternoon sun. The lemon tree grew and grew and produced an abundance of lemons. When we would cut a lemon off the tree we always said, "This is a gift from Ririka."

Salads

The Old Theater
CORFU, GREECE
From a photograph by Alice Padova Anderson

SALADS

Greek salads are simple and are made with fresh vegetables. The Greek salad made from leaf lettuce is a good example. Add to it feta cheese, slices of green peppers, tomatoes, cucumbers, and you have a very colorful village salad (Horiatiki).

Olive oil and lemon juice or olive oil and vinegar are the usual dressings. Many of the salads tend to be a one-vegetable salad (beet salad, zucchini salad, fresh bean salad). A favorite salad is boiled wild greens which are very popular certain times of the year. The locals will travel to the countryside to gather those greens by hand. A dish of boiled greens with lots of oil and lemon juice can be the main dish for supper accompanied by olives or feta cheese, potatoes, a boiled egg and lots of bread for dipping.

You can find other Greek salads with more ingredients but wc tend to mix fewer ingredients than in the United States.

GREENS AS SALAD

Greeks use boiled greens as a salad. Wild vegetables are very popular. Spinach, endive and Swiss chard can also be used. Boil the vegetables in salted water until tender. Drain and serve with olive oil and lemon juice or vinegar. It is customary to drink the broth separately with lemon juice.

BEAN SALAD

Makes 4 servings

1 pound Northern beans cooked
1/4 cup oil
1 small onion sliced
1/4 to 1/2 cup parsley chopped
Juice of 1 lemon
Salt and pepper

For garnish
1 tomato cut into wedges
Olives whole or sliced

Cook beans until done. Beans have to be tender but not mushy. Drain juice. Put on a platter. Mix with oil, lemon juice, onion and parsley. Garnish with tomato wedges and olives.

ZUCCHINI SALAD

Use small zucchini. Cook for 10-15 minutes in salted water. Drain. Serve them whole or cut into thick pieces. Add oil and vinegar or oil and lemon juice.

The flowers of the zucchini are edible. Separate them from the zucchini. Drop them into a thick batter and fry them quickly in oil. They make a nice appetizer.

GREEK POTATO SALAD

Makes 3-4 servings

2 pounds potatoes

1 onion finely chopped

2 tablespoons olive oil

1-2 teaspoons vinegar or lemon juice

1/4 - 1/2 cup chopped parsley

Salt and pepper

Boil the potatoes in their skins. Don't overcook. When cool enough, remove skins and cut potatoes into cubes. Add the onion and parsley. While hot, pour the oil and vinegar over them and season. Served cold, it goes well with fried fish.

EGGPLANT SALAD (MELITZANOSALATA)

Makes 4 servings

1 large eggplant

2-3 cloves of garlic chopped

1 cup chopped fresh parsley

2 small tomatoes peeled and chopped or 3 canned tomatoes peeled, drained and chopped

1/4 cup oil or more

3 tablespoons red wine vinegar

1-2 teaspoons oregano

Salt and pepper to taste

1/4 cup or more bread crumbs to absorb liquid

Place eggplant in a baking pan. Prick it in a few places to allow the steam to be released. If not, it will explode. Bake for 40 minutes at 475° until eggplant is soft. Open eggplant and scoop out the inside, discarding excess seeds.

Chop up eggplant and place it in a bowl. Add the garlic and parsley. Work the mixture well with a wooden spoon. Add the tomatoes, oil, vinegar, seasoning and mix them well. Add the bread crumbs to absorb the liquid.

The eggplant salad has to be thick and well-blended. Serve it as an appetizer with bread, crackers, or peta bread, or serve it on lettuce.

Use a blender if you like a smooth texture. Use lemon juice instead of vinegar if you prefer.

Because eggplants grow in a variety of sizes and weights, and because tastes vary from person to person , you might want to adjust the seasonings to your taste.

FISH ROE SALAD (TARAMOSALATA)

Makes 4-6 servings

4 slices of Italian or French bread (crust removed) soaked in water and squeezed dry

2 ounces fish roe (tarama)

1/2 cup oil

1/2 onion grated

Juice of 1 lemon

Cut bread into slices and let dry before using it. If fresh, it does not blend well.

In a mortar, blend tarama with bread to form a paste. Add the onion and small amounts of oil and lemon alternately, stirring well until mixture acquires a uniform smooth consistency. It needs to be pale pink in color, light and fluffy. Serve in a bowl garnished with parsley and olives.

Taramas can be served as an appetizer eaten with bread or crackers or it can accompany other food such as beets, green beans, fish or meat.

Taramosalata can be made with potatoes. Substitute the bread with one medium potato boiled and peeled.

For quick preparation, use a blender.

NOTE: You can find tarama in Greek or Middle Eastern stores.

BEET SALAD

Makes 4-6 servings

2 pounds beets
4 tablespoons oil
4-5 tablespoons vinegar
Salt and pepper

Separate the beet roots from the tops. Boil them separately because they have different cooking times. Boil the tops for 15 minutes and the roots 30 minutes or until they are tender but firm. Peel and slice the roots. Add oil and vinegar. The tops generally accompany the roots. Serve with fish and garlic sauce.

VILLAGE SALAD (HORIATIKI)

Makes 4-6 servings

3 tomatoes sliced
1 small cucumber sliced
1 onion chopped or sliced in rings
1 bell pepper
5-6 ounces olives
8 ounces feta cheese
4 tablespoons olive oil
2-3 tablespoons vinegar
2 tablespoons capers (optional)

Oregano

Salt and pepper to taste

Cut tomatoes and cucumber into slices. Cut onions and peppers into rounds. Mix together. Add oil, vinegar, and oregano. Lastly, add feta cheese broken into small chunks. Garnish with parsley and olives.

GREEK TOSSED SALAD

Servings depend on size of the lettuce

One head of leaf lettuce finely chopped into 1/4-inch strips

3-4 green onions sliced

Equal amounts of oil and vinegar or lemon juice

Olives for decoration

Seasoning to taste, salt, pepper, garlic salt and oregano.

Beat the oil and lemon juice until creamy. Fold into the salad. Add other fresh vegetables if you wish. Cucumbers, peppers, and tomatoes are most commonly used. If feta cheese is added, then it becomes a village salad (horiatiki).

RUSSIAN SALAD

Makes 10 servings or more

4 cups cooked vegetables or 20-ounce package frozen vegetables cooked (green beans, carrots, peas, etc.)

1 cup cooked beets sliced

2 cups boiled potatoes cubed

2-3 fresh green onions chopped

2 tablespoons capers

2 tablespoons parsley chopped

1-2 cups mayonnaise

Vinegar or lemon juice to taste

Salt and pepper to taste

Optional ingredients:

1 cup cooked beans, your choice

Sour pickle cut into small pieces

Lettuce leaves

Dill

For decoration:

3 hard-boiled eggs

Tomato wedges

Whole olives

Cook mixed vegetables. Green beans, peas and carrots can be cooked separately, but I find it easier to use a mixture of vegetables. Cook beets and slice. Cook potatoes and slice or cube. Combine cooked vegetables. Season with salt

and pepper. Add potatoes, beets, onions, capers and herbs. Fold in the mayonnaise until vegetables are mixed and well-coated.

Arrange in a serving bowl. Decorate with eggs, (slices or wedges) tomato wedges and olives. Make your own decoration.

Beets will add color to the salad. If a white salad is preferred, omit the beets or cut down the quantity.

GREEN BEAN SALAD

Makes 4 servings

2 pounds green beans

Vinegar

Oil

Clean green beans. Cut off ends with sharp knife. Boil them in salted water in an uncovered pan for 10-15 minutes. The pot is kept uncovered so that the beans won't lose their color. Drain and place them in a bowl. Add vinegar and oil and garnish with tomato wedges and olives.

Serve with fried fish.

SALADS

BAKED PEPPERS

Makes 4 servings

4 large bell peppers

4 cloves of garlic minced

1/2 cup of parsley chopped

Oil

2 tablespoons vinegar

Salt to taste

Cut peppers in half. Remove seeds. Bake in a hot oven until skin is black and you can separate it from the pulp.

Remove skins. Mix pulp with minced garlic and chopped parsley. Add oil, vinegar and salt. Serve it as a salad. Blend it in a blender if a dip is desirable.

Main Dish Pies

Statue of Adams in Front of Palace
CORFU, GREECE
From a photograph by Alice Padova Anderson

MAIN DISH PIES

There are many different ways to make a pie. I prefer making a thick béchamel sauce and adding different ingredients to it. I use it in cheese, spinach, leek, zucchini and eggplant pies. My version is similar to a souffle.

Of course, pies can be made without the sauce but still including different kinds of cheeses such as feta, kefalotyri and cottage cheese. Eggs, onions and vegetable seasonings can also be used. I have included a few pies under appetizers.

Commercial phyllo can be used or you can make your own pastry sheets, which takes patience and skill.

See homemade phyllo recipe on page 191.

CHEESE PIE (TYROPETA)

Makes 12 servings

Basic Sauce *Makes 5 cups sauce*

4 cups milk

6-8 tablespoons flour per cup

6 tablespoons butter

4 eggs beaten

Salt and pepper to taste

Melt butter in saucepan. Gradually add flour, stirring constantly. Slowly pour in the milk. Continue stirring until the sauce thickens. Add seasoning. If the sauce is lumpy use a whisk to break up the lumps and continue stirring. Break the eggs. Slightly beat them and pour them into the sauce. Then remove from fire.

Filling

8-12 ounces feta cheese

8 ounces mozzarella cheese

1/2 to 2/3 pound phyllo sheets

3/4 cup melted butter to spread on phyllo

Make the basic sauce. Crumble the feta cheese or cut it into small pieces. Add the feta and mozzarella cheeses. Mix well. There are two ways to combine the sauce with the phyllo.

1. Line the pan with half the pastry sheets, brushing each one with melted butter. Pour in the cheese filling and cover with the remaining pastry

sheets, brushing each one with the melted butter.

2. Line pan with 4-5 pastry sheets, brushing each one with melted butter. Add a small amount of cheese filling. Cover with a couple of pastry sheets brushed with butter. Repeat the procedure until the filling is finished. Generally the filling will cover 3-4 layers.

BOTH: Brush the top with the remaining butter. With a sharp knife, cut the top sheets into 3-inch squares. Bake in a moderate oven at 350° for 45 minutes to 1 hour until golden brown. Cut into squares and serve hot or cold. It can be frozen and reheated.

CHICKEN PIE (KOTOPETA)

Makes 12 servings

1 medium chicken

2 stalks celery diced

8 ounces feta cheese

8 ounces Parmesan cheese

Nutmeg

Phyllo

Butter for buttering phyllo

Basic Sauce (Follow the recipe on page 62.)

Boil the chicken. Dispose of the skin, remove meat from the bones, finely flake the meat. Prepare sauce. Add the chicken, cheeses, celery and nutmeg to the sauce. For assembling the pie, follow the preceding Cheese Pie recipe.

EGGPLANT PIE

Makes 12 servings

Basic Sauce (Follow the recipe on page 62.)

Filling

1 large eggplant
Oil for frying
Salt and pepper to taste
1/2 pound phyllo
Butter

Cut off ends of the eggplant and discard. Slice eggplant into half-inch slices. Heat the oil and fry eggplants until golden brown. Be aware that eggplants will absorb a lot of oil. In order to reduce the oil that is absorbed, use the following method. Take one slice at a time and coat it with flour. Quickly dip it into water and fry. The flour and water will create a coating around the eggplant and minimize the amount of oil absorbed. Place fried eggplants on paper towels to absorb any extra oil.

In a 9 x 13 pan, layer half the phyllo sheets buttered individually. Pour half of prepared sauce over the phyllo sheets and cover with a layer of eggplant slices. Pour the other half of the sauce on top. Finish with the remaining phyllo sheets buttered individually. Butter the top sheet. Carve the top sheets into 12 squares. Bake at 350° for one hour or until golden brown. When it cools, cut it into individual servings.

VARIATION: Eggplant pie with tomato sauce

An eggplant pie can be made with a sauce of eggplant, peppers, onion, tomato sauce, tomatoes, mushrooms and feta cheese, which you put between layers of phyllo and bake.

LEEK PIE

Makes 12 servings

Basic Sauce (Follow the recipe on page 62.)

Filling

4 pounds leeks

8 ounces feta cheese

8 ounces Parmesan or Kefalotyri cheese

20 sheets phyllo pastry

1 tablespoon dry dill or freshly chopped

Salt and pepper to taste

Butter for buttering phyllo

Use only the white parts of leeks. Cut roots and coarse tops and peel off the outer layers. Wash and clean leeks. Cut into 1 - 2-inch-thick slices. Before adding leeks to the sauce, shred and sauté them.

Prepare sauce. Add cheeses and seasonings. Follow directions for Tyropeta on pages 62 and 63 to assemble the pie.

Bake 45 minutes to one hour in a moderate oven

For a sharper taste, add more feta cheese.

LAMB PIE (ARNOPETA)

Makes 12 servings

2 pounds ground lamb
3/4 pound feta cheese
1 cup milk
4 eggs
1/2 cup rice
2-4 green onions chopped
4 tablespoons of chopped parsley
1/2 teaspoon cinnamon
Salt and pepper to taste
Oil for browning
1/2 pound phyllo sheets
Butter for the phyllo

Brown the ground lamb with oil. Add a little water and let it boil. Add the green onions and parsley and let it cook for 5-10 minutes. Add the rice and let meat and rice cook together for another 10 minutes. For better results, soak the rice in water for 15 minutes before adding to the meat. When the mixture is cool, add the cinnamon, the feta cheese mixed in milk and the 4 eggs, beaten. Season with salt and pepper. Prepare phyllo sheets by buttering them and laying half of them in a 9 x 13 pan. Pour the mixture on top of the phyllo sheets. Top with the remainder of the buttered phyllo sheets. Bake at a moderate temperature for 45 minutes to one hour. Let it cool for at least half an hour before cutting.

My mother's recipe book has three more lamb pie variations named after the people who gave her the recipes. There was Lamb Pie Markos, Lamb Pie Aglaia and Lamb Pie Ivi.

In her main black recipe book my mother referred to this meal as a lamb pie from Paxos Island. Paxos is a small island south of Corfu.

Her recipe called for six more eggs that she would beat with a little water and pour between the phyllo sheets. I have eliminated the extra eggs because of health reasons.

I decided to include the Paxos recipe because I made it in one of my cooking classes and the participants enjoyed it very much.

COD PIE

Makes 8-10 servings

2 pounds salted cod

1 cup rice

2 cups milk

Salt and pepper

Make a thick batter with:

Flour

Water

Oil

Salt and pepper to taste.

Soak dried cod in water for 24 hours, changing water 2-3 times. Drain. Remove the skin and bones.

Oil or butter a 9 x 13 pan. Spread the rice evenly. Cut cod into small bites. Dip the pieces into

In Corfu we make this pie without phyllo. Traditionally it is prepared the last Sunday of the Carnival prior to Lent.

the flour batter and arrange them on top of the rice. Pour the milk over the cod and bake in a moderate oven at 350° until the liquid is absorbed and rice is done. If necessary, add some more milk and/or water.

It is important to always keep the proportions of one part rice to two parts liquid.

SPINACH PIE (SPANAKOPETA)

Makes 12 servings

Basic Sauce (Follow the recipe on page 62.)

Filling

8-12 ounces feta cheese

8 ounces mozzarella

1/2 pound phyllo sheets

Butter for buttering phyllo

Two 10-ounce packages of frozen spinach

Dill weed, fresh or dried

Prepare the sauce. Add the thawed and squeezed spinach. Add the cheeses and dill weed. Dill weed will provide a unique flavor to the spinach.

Line a 9 x 13 pan with half the buttered phyllo sheets. Pour in the spinach pie filling. Top with the remaining pastry sheets brushed with melted butter. With a sharp knife, score the top sheets into 12 squares. Bake in moderate oven for 45 minutes to one hour. Let it cool and cut into pieces.

ZUCCHINI PIE

Makes 12 servings

Basic Sauce (Follow the recipe on page 62.)

Filling

2 pounds zucchini (4 medium size)
1 small onion finely chopped
Oil for frying
8 ounces feta cheese crumbled
Salt and pepper to taste
1/2 pound phyllo sheets
Butter for buttering phyllo

Sauté onion in oil. Put it aside. Slice zucchini into 1/4 inch rounds and fry in oil until brown on both sides. Place slices on paper towels to absorb the extra oil. Season while hot.

Prepare the sauce. Fold in the zucchini rounds and sautéed onion. Assemble the pie following the directions for Tyropeta on pages 62 and 63. Bake at 350° for 45 minutes to one hour. Serve hot or cold.

At times, I have used oil instead of butter to brush the phyllo pastries. I have done this for heath reasons. It can be done, but the butter provides more flavor.

SQUASH PIE

Makes 12 servings

Maria, a village woman, said that she made this recipe with all kinds of squash; summer squash, winter squash, yellow or orange squash. One time, she gave us a large and heavy squash the size of a small pumpkin, except that the consistency was much more that of butternut squash.

The following recipe provides the opportunity to experiment with your own garden squash. This recipe assumes the use of yellow squash or zucchini.

This recipe was given to me by Maria, one of the women in a Corfu village. She told me that it was necessary to invent a recipe because she had so many squashes in her garden.

4 cups grated squash (yellow squash or zucchini)
4 cups grated potatoes
1 cup cooked rice
3 eggs
8 ounces feta cheese
4 ounces Parmesan cheese
1 tablespoon oil
1/4 cup minced parsley
2 tablespoons minced dill
1/2 cup breadcrumbs
1/2 cup milk
Flour if needed
3/4 pound phyllo
Butter for brushing phyllo

Peel potatoes. Grate potatoes and squash coarse-

ly. Place them for 1/2 hour in a colander allowing the liquid to drain. In a large bowl, mix potatoes and squash. Beat eggs and add to the mixture. Crumble the feta cheese and add with all the other ingredients. Mix well.

Butter a 9 x 13 pan. Lay 5-6 phyllo sheets in the bottom, buttering each one individually. Pour the mixture into the pan and spread evenly. Top it with the remaining phyllo sheets. Butter one sheet at a time and butter the top sheet. With a sharp knife, score the top sheets into 12 squares. Bake at 350° for 1 hour or until liquid is absorbed. Serve cold.

VEGETABLE PIE (HORTOPETA)

Makes 12 squares

A vegetable pie can be made with cultivated or wild vegetables or a combination of both. Each vegetable contributes a unique flavor to the taste of the pie.

Here in the United States, I have used a combination of Swiss chard as my primary vegetable, while adding dandelion greens for a bitter taste and additional greens including spinach, escarole and mustard.

2 pounds of selected green vegetables
2 tablespoons parsley minced
1 tablespoon fennel leaves or dill minced

1 large onion sliced
1/4 to 1/2 cup of oil (used for sautéing and brushing the pastry sheets)
8 ounces feta cheese
3 eggs beaten
1/4 cup or more of milk
1/4 cup cooked rice
Salt and pepper to taste
1/2 to 3/4 pound phyllo

Cut the vegetables and herbs into pieces. Sauté in oil until they shrink in size. Some cooks boil the vegetables for 3 minutes. Drain and cut into pieces. Mince the vegetables, slice the onions, crumble the feta cheese and beat the eggs. Add the above ingredients plus the milk and rice to the sautéed vegetables. Mix well.

Line a 9 x 13-inch pan with 4-5 sheets of phyllo. Brush each one with oil. Pour in the filling evenly. Top with 4-5 more pastry sheets, oiling each one individually. Instead of one layer, you may decide to use two layers. Divide the filling in two and put a couple of phyllo sheets in between.

With a sharp knife, score the top layers of the phyllo. Bake at 350° for 40-45 minutes until the pastry is golden brown. Let it cool and cut.

There are so many wild greens found on Corfu Island that I cannot begin to name them all. Our housekeeper, Kiki, is an expert in this area. So, I always let her make the vegetable selection.

Grains & Pasta

Horse and Carriage
CORFU, GREECE

GRAINS & PASTA

Pasta is very popular on the island and it comes in all sizes and shapes. Macaroni is the most popular of all. In fact, years ago, Corfu had a pasta factory.

Many restaurants specialize in pasta dishes and toppings. Pastas are served as the first dish or they accompany meat and fish dishes. Kritharaki, a type of orzo, is also very popular with lamb and beef casseroles. Rice is used in stuffing dolmades, stuffed tomatoes and stuffed zucchini. Rice is also used in soups and risotto-like dishes.

Bulgur and cracked wheat, used in making pilafs and soups, were staples in my family.

Another popular dish in my family was boiled whole wheat with raisins, nuts and sugar. We ate it as a side dish or dessert.

This dish, called Kolyva, originated with the Greek Orthodox Church tradition. Forty days after the death of a family member, the family takes a tray of boiled wheat, white raisins, Jordanian almonds, spices and sugar to the church. The dish is then blessed by the priest during the memorial service. At the end of the service the food is distributed among the faithful. The tradition holds that the family prepare the dish again at the end of the first and third years following the death.

GRAINS & PASTA

BAKED MACARONI WITH MEAT SAUCE (PASTITSIO)

Makes 8-12 servings

2 pounds macaroni (other tubular pasta can be used, such as ziti)
1 1/2 pounds ground meat
2 medium onions finely diced
2 cloves minced garlic
1 teaspoon dried oregano
1/2 teaspoon cinnamon
Salt and pepper to taste
2 cups Italian tomatoes chopped
1 cup tomato sauce or 8-ounce can
1 1/4 cups oil (or less)
1 cup grated Parmesan or other hard cheese
1/2 cup bread crumbs

Béchamel Sauce
4 cups milk
1 cup flour (more for a thicker sauce)
3 eggs beaten
1 stick butter
5-6 ounces of Parmesan or Kefalotyri cheese
Salt and pepper to taste
1/4 teaspoon nutmeg (optional)

In salted water cook the macaroni al dente. Drain and put aside in cold water. In a

saucepan, using 2-4 tablespoons oil, sauté onions until they become a golden color. Brown the meat with the onions and add the garlic, oregano, cinnamon, salt and pepper. Drain the fat from the meat before seasoning it. Add the diced tomatoes and the tomato sauce and cook for about 30 minutes until the sauce thickens. In a saucepan, heat the remaining oil and pour over the drained macaroni. If this is too much oil for you, use less. Add the cheese and mix well.

In a deep baking pan, place a layer of macaroni and cover it with the meat sauce. Top it with another layer of macaroni and cover it with a béchamel sauce. Sprinkle bread crumbs on top. Bake at 350° for 30 minutes or more until golden brown. Let cool for half an hour. Cut into squares.

For the sauce: Heat the oil and add the flour, stirring constantly. Heat the milk and pour it slowly into the mixture. When it thickens, remove from fire and add the beaten eggs, seasoning, nutmeg and the cheese while stirring constantly.

For a thicker sauce, add more flour and less milk. If the sauce is too thick, add a little more milk.

VARIATION: In Corfu we make pastitsio with phyllo. Place four phyllo sheets on the bottom of the pan, the macaroni and meat sauce in the middle, and a few phyllo sheets on top. Do not use the béchamel sauce with this variation.

CRACKED WHEAT PILAF

Makes 4-6 servings

1 cup cracked wheat
2 cups water
2 tablespoons oil
1/2 onion chopped

Sauté onion in the oil. Add the cracked wheat and stir vigorously so the oil will be absorbed. Add water and let it simmer for 10-15 minutes, stirring occasionally until the liquid is absorbed. If a softer pilaf is desired, add some water, but in small amounts, so that the mixture does not become mushy.

Though slightly different, bulgur may be substituted for the cracked wheat. Bulgur is made from wheat berries that are boiled, dried and cracked.

This is what my mother called rizotto. Don't confuse this recipe with the Italian Rizotto for which a special type of rice and special preparation procedures are required.

RICE WITH TOMATO SAUCE MOTHER'S RIZOTTO

Makes 4 servings

1 cup rice
2 cups water
2 tablespoons tomato paste
2 tablespoons oil
1/2 medium onion chopped
Salt and pepper to taste

Dissolve the tomato paste in a little water. Add

to the rest of the water. Add the chopped onion, oil and rice. Cook for 10 minutes in a covered pan. Lower the heat and simmer, covered, for another 10 minutes. Shut off the heat but leave it on the burner for an additional 10 minutes until the liquid is absorbed.

Serve with grated Parmesan or crumbled feta cheese as a side or a main dish.

POLENTA (POULENTA)

Makes 4-6 servings

5 cups water

1 1/2 cups cornmeal

Salt to taste

Pour four cups of water into a pan and bring to a boil. Combine the cornmeal with the other cup of water and mix until uniform. Slowly pour the cornmeal mixture into the boiling water. Add salt and stir with a wooden spoon until it thickens to the consistency of a soup. Stir the mixture occasionally. If the heat is too high, the mixture will bubble vigorously.

In Corfu, we serve polenta in a soup plate and top it with some olive oil. I grew up on polenta. My mother served it at least once a week. Tzia Kerkyra, my great-aunt, would add four tablespoons of tomato sauce or two tablespoons of tomato paste which made it pink. Before sitting down for the meal, I would ask if yellow or pink polenta was being served.

In my family, we made polenta into a soup that was not too thick, and we never baked it.

By adding nuts, raisins and some milk to the cornmeal mixture, we created a polenta pudding dessert.

MACARONI AU GRATIN

Makes 10-12 servings

2 pounds macaroni
4 eggs
2 cups milk
1/2 cup butter melted
1 cup Parmesan cheese grated
1/2 to 3/4 cup breadcrumbs

White Sauce
2 cups milk
1/2 stick of butter
4 tablespoons of flour or more for a thicker sauce

Prepare macaroni al dente. Do not overcook. Cool macaroni in cold water. Drain. Pour into large mixing bowl. Add the melted butter and grated cheese. Mix well with a wooden spoon. Beat eggs separately and add milk to the eggs. Butter a 9 x 13 pan. Pour in the buttered macaroni and add the egg-milk mixture. The macaroni will absorb the milk and will become softer and fluffier. Sprinkle the macaroni with bread crumbs and pour white sauce over the top.

Bake at 350° until golden brown.

Sauces & Dressings

The Old Castle
CORFU, GREECE

SAUCES & DRESSINGS

Olive oil is the main ingredient for many of the Greek sauces and dressings. It is used for salads and boiled greens. Oftentimes it is mixed with lemon juice or vinegar and a number of herbs such as oregano, mint and dill. The island of Corfu is a producer of oil. Thousands of olive trees were planted during the Venetian occupation. Venetians promoted the cultivation of olive trees and paid the peasants a certain amount of money for every tree planted.

Other typical Greek sauces include avgolemono, which is a tart and creamy sauce made with eggs and lemon juice. It is added to soups and stews. It is also served with a number of vegetable dishes.

Tomato sauce is used with many meats, poultry and vegetable dishes.

A garlic saucc called skordalia is made out of garlic, mashed potatoes and lots of olive oil. It is a strong and aromatic sauce used with fish, beets, cucumbers, eggplants and fresh beans.

The white sauce we call béchamel has eggs in it. It is used for topping moussaka and pastitsio.

In the sauces, Greeks have traditionally used ingredients that are plentiful in nature.

GARLIC SAUCE (SKORDALIA)

Skordalia is popular among the Greeks. It can be used in a variety of food combinations, as a dip or as a side dish. The sauce goes well with fried fish, fried eggplant and squash, boiled beets, green beans and other vegetables. In my house we used to have fried cod, garlic sauce, and green beans.

6 - 8 cloves garlic minced
4 boiled potatoes mashed
1 cup olive oil
Juice of 1 lemon
Salt to taste
1/4 to 1/2 cup water

Garlic can be minced or put through a mincer. Then put it in a mortar and pound until very smooth. Add the mashed potatoes. Blend to a soft paste. Alternately add the oil and lemon juice slowly. Make sure it is fully absorbed before more is added. Stir in water until it is absorbed.

VARIATIONS: Bread can be used instead of potatoes. Use 6 slices of white bread, crusts removed. Soak bread in water and squeeze it dry.

Use vinegar instead of lemon. I prefer lemon.

I have seen cooks use more oil. I would not recommend it. More oil makes a heavy sauce.

If you wish to make a lighter skordalia, use less garlic and add more water. If a strong garlic sauce is preferred, use less potatoes and more garlic. However, the consistency must stay the same. It has to be a thick, creamy sauce.

Using a mixer or food processor is quicker, but some cooks don't like it because it changes the consistency of the sauce. The trick to a smooth

EGGPLANT SPAGHETTI SAUCE

1 medium eggplant
1 large pepper chopped
1 medium onion sliced
2-4 tablespoons oil
1 can stewed tomatoes (14-16 ounces)
1 can tomato sauce (8 ounces)
1 tablespoon oregano
1/2 cup chopped parsley
Salt and pepper to taste

Cut the eggplant in cubes and boil until tender. Drain and set aside. Sauté onion in oil. Add the pepper and sauté with the onion for five more minutes. Add all the other ingredients and cook for half an hour. Simmer for another half hour or more until the ingredients have blended and liquid has been absorbed. Stir occasionally. Add some water if needed. Generally, the eggplant cubes will absorb the water but sometimes not. Add tap water or some of the eggplant liquid if you like the bitter taste. Add sauce to spaghetti or other pasta.

NOTE: For a spicy sauce add the following:
1 bay leaf
1/2 teaspoon cinnamon
1/4 teaspoon cloves

In many of the recipes, I am suggesting quantities of oil. In my experience, Greeks use more oil than Americans. If you desire to use more oil, it can be added during any stage of cooking. First, try the dish to find out how it tastes to you.

OLIVE OIL AND LEMON JUICE DRESSING (LADOLEMONO)

Use equal amounts of olive oil and lemon juice. Beat olive oil and lemon juice until creamy. Add salt and pepper and your favorite herb such as oregano, mint or parsley.

This dressing can be used for fresh salads, green vegetables, broiled fish and shellfish.

EGG-LEMON SAUCE (AVGOLEMONO)

2 eggs
Juice of 1 - 2 lemons
1 cup chicken stock or broth from the food in which the sauce is going to be used
Salt and pepper

Warm the broth.

In a bowl, beat the eggs until frothy. Add the lemon juice. Continue beating. Gradually add the warm broth, beating continually. Simmer over low heat (don't boil) until mixture has thickened. If added to a soup, stir constantly with a wooden spoon. If added to meat or vegetables, shake the saucepan. It is ready when the sauce coats the dipping spoon and the side of the pan. Don't overcook.

This sauce is very popular in Greece. It is added to soups, stews, vegetables and meats.

OLIVE OIL AND VINEGAR DRESSING

Mix equal amounts of olive oil and vinegar. Beat well. Add seasoning to taste. Pour over fresh or cooked salads.

I use this dressing for lettuce salad. If I want a sharper taste, I use more vinegar. Oregano is my choice of herb.

VARIATION: Use equal amounts of olive oil, vinegar and lemon juice.

BÉCHAMEL SAUCE

This is a white sauce with eggs. This is a basic recipe. You will find many variations including other ingredients.

6 tablespoons butter

4 cups milk

4 - 6 tablespoons of flour for every cup of milk

2 - 3 eggs slightly beaten

Salt and pepper to taste

Melt butter in a saucepan. Gradually add flour while stirring constantly. Pour in the hot milk slowly. Continue stirring until the sauce thickens. Add salt and pepper. Beat eggs and fold them into the sauce. If you want a thicker sauce, use the higher amount of flour.

Béchamel sauce is used in a number of Greek dishes. It is used as a topping for pastitsio and moussaka. Parmesan or other hard cheese can be sprinkled on top. The sauce is also used as filling for cheese pies and vegetable pies. Cheeses are added to these recipes. (See recipes on pages 62 and 71).

TOMATO SAUCE

2 pounds tomatoes chopped
1 medium onion chopped
1/2 cup oil
1/4 cup red wine
3/4 to 1 cup water
1/2 teaspoon cinnamon or a cinnamon stick
1 bay leaf
Salt and pepper

Sauté onion in oil for 5 minutes. Add chopped tomatoes and sauté them with the oil. Let them wilt. Add watcr, the bay leaf and the seasonings. Let simmer for 30 minutes or more, until water is absorbed. If needed, add more water. Add wine at the end of cooking and allow it to be absorbed. Discard the bay leaf and cinnamon stick. Serve with macaroni or spaghetti.

For variety, use other seasonings such as fresh or dried oregano, basil, dill, mint or rosemary. A few cloves of garlic can also be added.

Beef & Pork, Lamb, Rabbit & Ground Meat

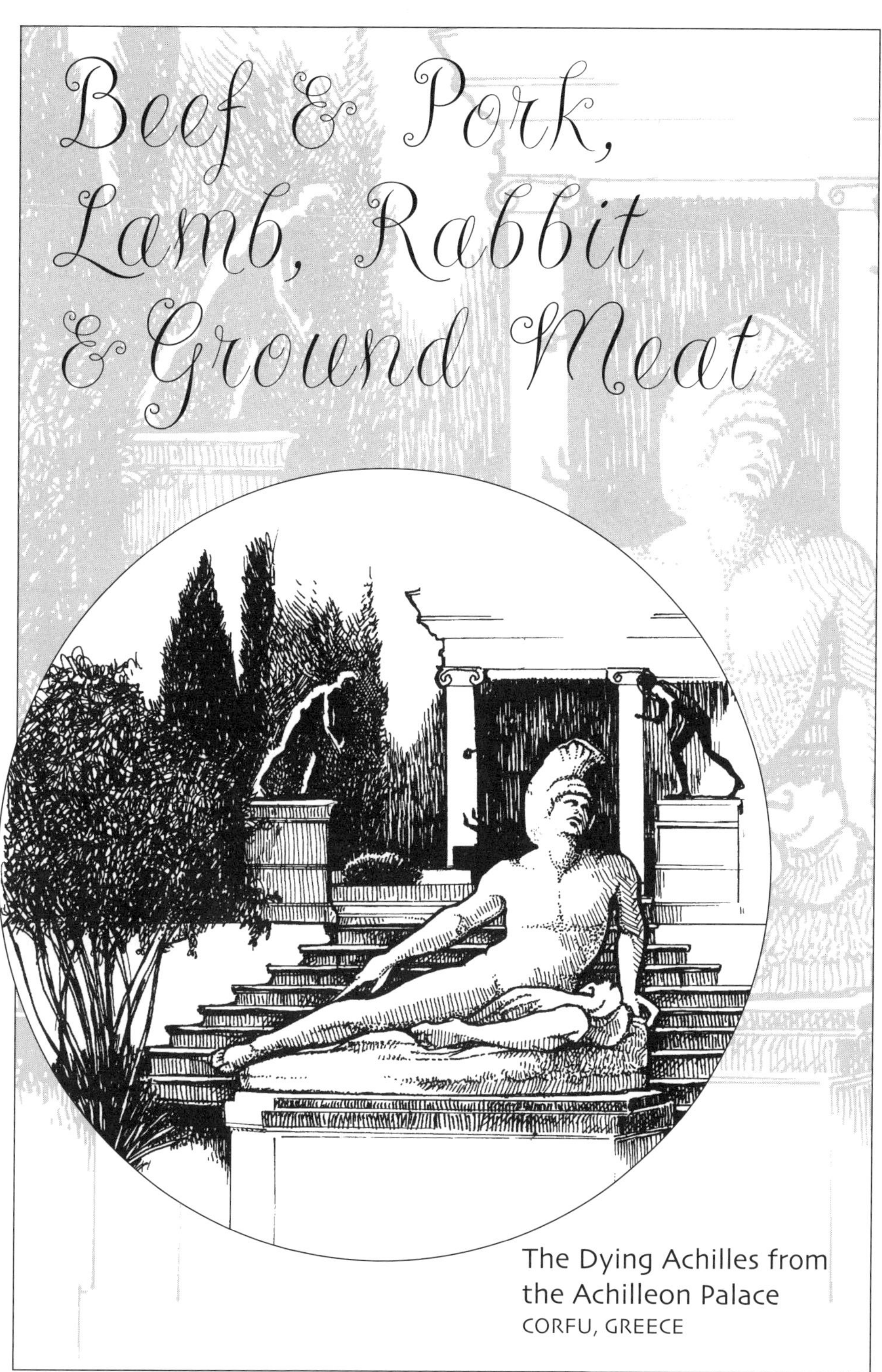

The Dying Achilles from the Achilleon Palace
CORFU, GREECE

MEAT

BEEF & LAMB, PORK, RABBIT & GROUND MEAT

Our meat came from the animals we raised; sheep, poultry, rabbits and the occasional game.

We ate meat sparingly, once a week, and we always had our lamb for Easter. A spit-roasted lamb is the traditional food for Greek Easter holidays which follow a long fasting period. Lamb meat is used in many dishes because of its distinct flavor. Try a roasted leg of lamb, or lamb in a meat pie or moussaka.

You will find Kapama, Fricassee, and Stifado in both poultry and meat recipes. These are methods of cooking rather than a reference to the type of meat.

PASTITSADA

Makes 4-6 servings

2 pounds beef or veal
2 pounds ripe tomatoes peeled and finely chopped (4 medium)
3/4 cup oil
3 onions chopped
Dash of sugar
1 cup red wine
Salt, black pepper and red pepper to taste
1 teaspoon cinnamon
1/4 teaspoon cloves or whole cloves
1/4 teaspoon nutmeg
2-3 bay leaves

Cut the meat into pieces. Heat the oil in a pan and brown meat on all sides. Add chopped onions and fry until soft. Add the wine, the tomatoes and water to cover the meat. Let it cook over moderate heat for one hour. Then add the seasonings and sugar. Continue to cook for one more hour at moderate to low heat until the meat is tender and well cooked. The sauce should be thick and dark. If needed, add more water to avoid scorching.

After cooking, bay leaves and whole cloves can be removed from the dish.

Traditionally, pastitsada is served with macaroni and the sauce is mixed in with it.

The amount of spices is only a suggested amount. If you like a more spicy taste, increase the amounts. Always use cloves in lesser amounts than cinnamon because they tend to dominate the taste.

PSEUDO PASTITSADA

1 onion minced
3 cloves of garlic minced
1/4 to 1/2 cup oil
6-8 ounces of tomato sauce
Salt and pepper to taste
2 bay leaves
Cinnamon, cloves and nutmeg to taste

Sauté onions in oil for 5 minutes. Add 1/2 cup of water and cook until onions are tender. Add the garlic. Cook briefly. Add 2 cups of water, tomato sauce, seasoning and spices. Let it cook and absorb the water. Toward the end of cooking, add the 2 bay leaves.

In order to make the sauce light, Kiki boils the onion in water. When tender, discard the water and then sauté the cooked onion in oil. Continue the recipe as above.

This recipe was given to me by Kiki, our family helper. When she does not want to use meat, she uses this sauce to put on the macaroni. Generally, we use the sauce from the pastitsada. This sauce is much lighter.

PORK WITH CELERY IN EGG-LEMON SAUCE

Makes 4-6 servings

2 pounds pork
2 pounds celery
1/2 cup oil
2 onions chopped
2 tablespoons dill finely chopped
Salt and pepper to taste

Egg-Lemon Sauce

2 eggs
Juice of 2 lemons

Cut pork into serving pieces. Sauté the onions in oil. Add the meat with one cup of water and season. Allow the meat to simmer for one hour. Clean celery and cut into large pieces, 3-4 inches. For a more tender celery, boil in salted water for a few minutes and drain. Then add to the meat with the dill.

Let it cook with the meat for 35-40 minutes. When the meat is done, remove from heat. Make the egg-lemon sauce. Follow directions on page 86 and combine with the meat mixture.

PORK WITH QUINCE

Makes 5-6 servings

For this recipe, we generally use pork but you can use beef, lamb or poultry. Quince blends very well with any kind of meat.

3 pounds boneless meat cut into portions or cut into 2-inch cubes

2 onions chopped

4 tablespoons oil

4 pounds quince

Salt and pepper to taste

Pinch of cinnamon

Sugar

Sauté the onions and the meat in oil until the onions are soft and the meat is browned. Cover with water and simmer for about 1 hour or until the meat is cooked.

Meanwhile, core and peel the quince. Cut into slices. Put the slices in a bowl and sprinkle with sugar. Leave it for 30 minutes while the quince absorbs the sugar. Add quince to the meat. Pour any liquid left in the bowl into the pan with the meat. Add cinnamon, salt, pepper and more water if necessary. Continue to cook meat until it is tender and the quinces are soft. Cooking time is about one hour.

Quince is a fruit that is grown throughout Greece. It is shaped like a fat pear, yellow on the outside and white on the inside. It is very hard and has a tart taste. I occasionally find it in American groceries, but you have to be able to recognize it.

STEWED MEAT WITH ONIONS (STIFADO)

Makes 4-5 servings

2 pounds lean meat

16-20 small onions (The size used for planting. In Mother's recipe, she specifies 4-5 per person.)

1/2 to 1 cup red wine

2-3 bay leaves

2-3 cloves of garlic cut in half

1/2 to 3/4 cup oil

1 cup tomato sauce

Cinnamon

Salt and pepper to taste

Cut meat into 1 1/2 inch cubes. Brown meat in oil on all sides for 5 minutes. Stir with a large spoon to avoid sticking and scorching. Add onions and garlic and continue stirring for another 5 minutes. Prick onions with a fork or a knife so that they can absorb the oil. Add the wine, tomato sauce, cinnamon and seasoning and enough water to cover. Reduce heat and simmer over very low heat for 2 hours or more until meat is tender and the sauce is thick. Check it from time to time to see that the meat is not sticking to the pan. If it does, add some water.

Stifado is a very slow cooking stew. Cook it for a longer time than other entrees. Years ago, the cook would seal the pot with dough and open it only at

the end of cooking. Temperatures had to be extremely low.

If you don't have the very small onions, use the smallest onions you can find and quarter them.

VARIATION: Cook the carrots, celery or parsley separately. Cook the vegetables mainly in oil and add them to the stifado at the end of the cooking period.

SOFRITO

Makes 4-6 servings

2 pounds lean meat (beef or veal)
1/2 to 1 cup finely chopped parsley
6 cloves of garlic minced
1 cup dry red wine or a combination of wine and vinegar (3/4 wine to 1/4 vinegar)
2/3 cup oil
2 bay leaves
Flour
Salt and pepper to taste

Cut meat into thin slices. Pound with a mallet to tenderize. The slices of meat should be thin, 1/4 to 1/2 inch thick. The thinner the better. Flour and fry meat in oil until it is brown on all sides. Cover the meat with the wine, parsley, garlic, bay leaves and a little water. Season well with salt and pepper. Simmer until meat is tender and the liquid is reduced to a thick sauce.

Serve with mashed potatoes.

A specialty of Corfu. It is probably Venetian in origin.

Most of the Corfu dishes are peppery. Instead of black pepper, use some paprika or red pepper. Taste it for intensity.

Coco

My father had a special relationship with animals, a gift. He trained all kinds of animals. He was firm and loving and the animals always obeyed him. One year, my father trained a young rooster, named Pico, to fly onto his extended arm and eat out of his hand. Father would invite family and friends out into the garden and give repeated demonstrations of his training skills. Pico lived for a short time. One overcast day the bird flew into a nearby well and drowned. When the young rooster was discovered, I could see the sorrow in Father's eyes and hear it in his voice. He never trained another bird after that experience.

> "As a rooster general, he usually conceived and executed a well-planned offensive."

Father had no luck with a huge, red rooster who would proudly parade in front of his hens with his wings extended downward as if he was wearing colorful coattails. That rooster, named Coco, would defend his hens to the end and Coco would attack anyone who would enter the poultry enclosure. Coco was so mean that only a few family members would dare to venture into the enclosure. He would chase us out, leaving bloody peck marks on our legs. Coco would stay within the flock of hens until someone came into the enclosure. Then he would run after the intruder, viciously attacking bare legs or fly at the body using claws as weapons. Wooden sticks or brooms could not fend off Coco. As a rooster general, he usually conceived and executed a well-planned offensive.

Only Father was able to restrain that flying, lethal bird. He would enter the poultry yard and walk up to Coco. With the first provocation, Father would grab the rooster's neck with one hand while he restrained the bird's legs with his other hand. Father would then talk to him, saying, "I want this to stop. Do you hear me?" The talk was brief and forceful. He would then release Coco and walk away. If Coco attacked him from behind, Father would repeat the same procedure. Finally, Coco understood that he was no longer the dominant rooster. Father was the dominant male. But Coco continued to chase and inflict wounds on the other members of the family. Finally, my parents decided that another, less aggressive, rooster should take his place. And Coco was killed, cooked and served for Sunday dinner.

LAMB CASSEROLE WITH ORZO

2 - 3 pounds of boneless lamb
4 tablespoons olive oil
One medium onion minced
8-ounce can of tomato sauce
Salt and pepper to taste
8-8 1/2 cups of boiling water
1/2 pound orzo
1 cup Greek Kritharaki pasta
Parmesan or Kefalotyri cheese to serve on top

Cut the meat in small pieces. Brown meat in oil on all sides. Set it aside. Sauté onions for five minutes. Add tomato sauce and meat. Season with salt and pepper and add two cups of boiling water. Mix well. Transfer to a casserole dish. Cover and bake at 350° for one hour or until meat is tender. When done, add the pasta and 6 - 6 1/2 cups of boiling water. Stir well and bake for another one-half hour until liquid is absorbed. Serve hot with grated cheese on top.

LAMB FRICASSEE

LAMB WITH GREEN VEGETABLES AND EGG-LEMON SAUCE

Makes 4-6 servings

3 pounds of lamb cut into portions (beef can be substituted)

2 pounds of green vegetables (endive, spinach, wild greens)

4 green onions finely chopped

1/2 cup oil

1 tablespoon dry dill weed or two fresh sprigs

Salt and pepper to taste

Egg-Lemon Sauce

2 eggs

Juice of 2 lemons

2 teaspoons corn flour

In a saucepan, sauté onions in the oil until soft. Add the meat and sauté. Season with salt and pepper. Cover with water and simmer for 1 to 1 1/2 hours until the meat is half cooked. Clean, wash and drain vegetables and place them in the pot with the lamb. Vegetables can be cut into pieces or left whole. Sprinkle the dill weed on the vegetables or add the fresh dill. Simmer for 20-25 minutes until the liquid is absorbed. Remove from heat.

Make the egg-lemon sauce. In a bowl, beat the eggs with a fork until they are frothy. Add the

lemon juice and the corn flour diluted with some water. Slowly add broth from the pot, beating constantly. When most of the broth has been transferred to the bowl, pour the egg-lemon sauce over the food and remove from heat. Let it stand until it thickens. If you need to further thicken, place the pot over very low heat, shaking it until you get the desired consistency.

VARIATION: Two of my favorite vegetables for this dish are leeks and celery, which can be substituted for the greens. Generally one kind of vegetable is used for fricassee. The cook makes a choice.

With leeks: Use 2 pounds of leeks. Remove the outer tough leaves. Wash thoroughly to remove any soil or sand. Cut into pieces 2-3 inches long. Cook with the meat for 30 minutes.

With celery: Use one large bunch. Rinse well. Cut into 2-3 inch pieces. Use the leaves. Cook for 30 minutes with the meat.

In Greece, we use a kind of celery unique to the Mediterranean countries, which is called celeriac.

Try some other vegetables for yourself, fresh or frozen. Artichokes, cauliflower and broccoli are all possibilities.

LAMB WITH OKRA

Makes 4-5 servings

2 pounds lamb
2 pounds okra
2 onions finely chopped
2-4 tablespoons parsley finely chopped
1/2 cup oil
4-6 tablespoons vinegar
1 cup tomato sauce
1 cup water
Salt and pepper to taste

Cut meat into serving pieces. Brown meat in oil for 5 minutes. Add onions and sauté with the meat. Add tomato sauce, parsley, seasoning and water to cover meat. Simmer for 45 minutes to one hour until meat is tender.

Meanwhile, prepare okra by first cutting off the stems. Place okra in a bowl of water with salt and vinegar, and let it stand for 30 minutes. Before cooking, discard the gluey liquid. Rinse and drain.

Add the okra to the meat and cook together for another 30 minutes. If the dish needs more cooking, do so on a very low heat.

You can substitute beef for lamb.

LAMB WITH STRING BEANS

Makes 4-5 servings

2 pounds lamb
1/2 stick butter
2 onions minced
2 pounds string beans
1 cup tomato sauce
Salt and pepper to taste
2-4 tablespoons parsley minced
1 cup water

Cut meat into serving pieces. Brown meat in butter for five minutes. Add onions and sauté for another five minutes. Add the tomato sauce, parsley, seasoning and water to cover meat. Simmer for 45 minutes to one hour until meat is tender. Add beans and continue cooking for another 30 minutes. If the dish needs more cooking, continue cooking on low heat until done.

You can substitute beef for lamb.

LAMB

ROASTED LEG OF LAMB (ARNI PSITO)

Makes 5-6 servings

Leg or shoulder of lamb (4-5 pounds)
4-6 cloves of garlic
1/4 cup oil
1 cup water
Juice of 1 lemon
Salt and pepper
Some sliced potatoes

Wash lamb and place in roasting pan. Make incisions in the meat and insert cloves of garlic (whole cloves or sliced in half). Rub the entire roast with salt, pepper, oil and half the lemon juice.

Cook covered for one hour in the oven at 350°. Add one cup of water and baste roast during cooking. Continue cooking until it is tender and golden brown on all sides.

Add sliced potatoes the last 30 minutes of cooking. Sprinkle with oregano and add the rest of the lemon juice. You might need more water as potatoes absorb the liquid.

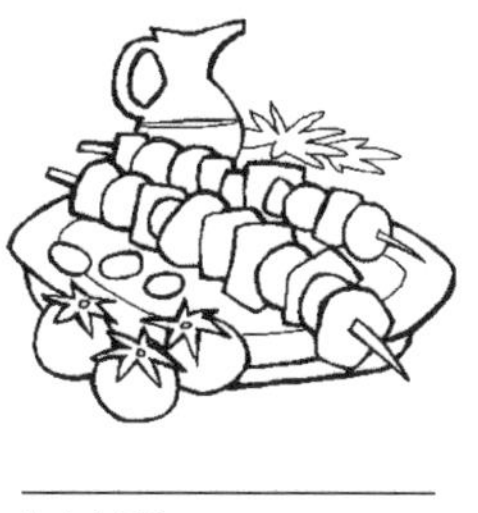

LAMB KAPAMA

Makes 4-5 servings

3 pounds lamb

1/4 cup oil

1 pound ripe tomatoes, or 1 15-16 ounce can sliced tomatoes

Juice of 4-5 lemons

Salt and pepper to taste

Cut the lamb into portions. Put it on a platter. Pour lemon juice on the meat. Allow to stand for one hour. Brown meat in oil, adding the extra lemon juice from the platter. Put meat in a saucepan with the tomatoes and seasoning. Cook slowly for 1 to 1 1/2 hours until the meat is tender and juices are absorbed.

Serve with pasta, rice or potatoes.

If you like cinnamon, add a pinch of cinnamon in the pan.

When you use fresh tomatoes, add 1 teaspoon of sugar to cut the acidity of the tomatoes.

Boulis the Ram

Boulis, the ram, was my father's pride and joy. I remember that the animal was majestic, proud and strong. Very soon after his birth, Boulis demonstrated the ability to respond to father's voice. Father would walk into the garden with a bucket of corn and call his name, and Boulis would come running. For months this arrangement worked very well. But as Boulis grew in size, he also grew in strength. When the ram would see us children, he would charge, reminding us that we had to give him food. Eventually, it became difficult to walk into the garden. We had to scamper from tree to tree to avoid the charging ram. For a while it was a game, but soon it became a problem. Mother, who was in charge of our orchard, spent hours grafting the trees. Frequently she had to fend off Boulis' attacks by positioning a stepping stool between her and the charging animal.

> "The end of Boulis came about when my grandfather ventured into the garden."

Boulis had another problem. One of his beautiful, curly horns grew inward, toward his head. Father sawed it off twice but it grew back quickly in the same direction. Boulis became a problem.

The end of Boulis came about when Grandfather ventured into the garden. Although the old man was cautious, the ram charged and knocked Grandfather to the ground. The ram then proceeded to charge him again. After that, Boulis had to go. At the time, my parents told me that Boulis was sent away to a village. But many years later, mother told me that I had eaten Boulis for lunch.

RABBIT WITH LEMON JUICE

Makes 6 servings

3 pound rabbit
Juice of 6-8 lemons
5 cloves garlic cut in pieces
3/4 - 1 cup oil
3/4 cup white wine
1 pound feta cheese crumbled
Salt and pepper to taste

Cut the rabbit into serving pieces and marinate in the juice of 3-4 lemons for twelve hours. In a saucepan, heat the oil and sauté the garlic. Add the rabbit and fry until golden brown. Then, add the wine and the juice from the remaining lemons. Add salt and pepper. Cook over low heat until meat is tender. When ready, add the crumbled feta cheese and turn off the heat.

RABBIT WITH TOMATO SAUCE

MARO'S RECIPE

Makes 6 servings

3 pounds rabbit
2 onions sliced
3 cloves garlic chopped
1/2 cup parsley chopped
1/2 cup oil
1 stick butter
1/2 cup white wine
2-4 tablespoons of tomato paste
Water

Cut rabbit into serving pieces. Sauté onions in an oil-butter mixture. Add garlic and parsley. Let them sauté for five minutes. Remove the ingredients with a spoon. Put the pieces of rabbit in the oil/butter combination. Fry until golden brown. Now, add the onions, garlic and parsley that were removed and add the wine. After the wine has been absorbed, cover with the water in which you have diluted the tomato paste. Continue to cook on low heat until rabbit is tender. Add more water if needed.

Serve with vegetables and/or mashed potatoes.

RABBIT STIFADO

Makes 6 servings

3 pound rabbit
12-14 small onions whole
4 cloves garlic minced
3 bay leaves
1 tablespoon rosemary
1 cup tomato sauce
1/2 cup oil
Salt and pepper to taste

Wash rabbit and cut into serving pieces. Brown meat in oil on all sides for five minutes. Add whole onions and garlic. If the small round onions are not available, use the smallest onions that can be found and quarter them. Add the oil, tomato sauce and seasonings. Cover with water and let simmer on a low heat for two hours or until rabbit is tender. Serve hot as a main dish.

VARIATION: If you want a spicy, sweet taste, add one cup raisins and substitute the bay leaves and rosemary for 1 teaspoon cinnamon, 1/4 teaspoon ground cloves and 1/2 teaspoon nutmeg.

RABBIT WITH OIL AND OREGANO

MOTHER'S LADORIGANI RABBIT

Makes 6 servings

3 pound rabbit

6-8 cloves garlic

10-12 pieces or cubes of hard cheese (Parmesan or Kefalotyri)

1 cup oil

Juice of 1-2 lemons

2 potatoes diced

2-3 small zucchini

1-2 carrots cut into pieces

Oregano to taste

Thyme to taste

Salt and pepper to taste

Cut rabbit into serving pieces. Salt and let them stand overnight. Next day, sauté in the oil. Add the whole garlic cloves and pieces of cheese. Sprinkle with oregano and thyme. Cover with water and lemon juice. Cook over moderate heat until rabbit is tender. Add water if necessary. When done, remove rabbit from pan. Add the potato, zucchini and carrots to the juice and cook over slow heat. When cooked, remove from pan, then place the rabbit back in the liquid a little longer so that it will absorb the juices. Serve in a dish accompanied by the vegetables.

GROUND MEAT

MEATBALLS IN EGG-LEMON SAUCE (GIOUVARLAKIA)

Makes 4-6 servings

2 pounds hamburger
2 small onions grated or minced
2 tablespoons chopped parsley
1 tablespoon chopped mint
2 eggs
1/2 cup rice
Salt and pepper to taste
1 quart water
Juice of 2 lemons

Fresh basil or dill can be used as a parsley substitute, or your own combination of favorite herbs.

Mix basic ingredients well. Shape the meat mixture into small round balls the size of a walnut.

Bring water to a boil. Drop the meatballs into the water while it is boiling. Reduce heat and allow meatballs to simmer for 30-40 minutes. Remove from heat. Prepare the egg-lemon sauce (see directions on page 86). Combine some of the broth with the egg-lemon mixture and pour over meatballs. Shake the pot so that the sauce spreads throughout the container. Do not boil after adding the sauce, because the sauce will separate. Use extremely low heat until the sauce thickens and shake the pot frequently.

GROUND MEAT

FRIED MEATBALLS

Makes 4-6 servings

2 pounds hamburger
2 medium onions minced
1/2 cup bread crumbs
2 eggs
1/4 cup oil
3-4 tablespoons parsley finely chopped
1 clove garlic minced
Salt and pepper to taste
Frying oil
Flour for coating

Mix all ingredients together well. Shape into small round balls. Coat with flour and fry in very hot oil until well-browned.

A substitute for bread crumbs can be 2 slices of bread dipped in milk and then mixed with the hamburger. This combination makes the mixture softer.

Small meatballs can bc used as appetizers.

MEATBALLS IN TOMATO SAUCE

Makes 4-6 servings

Follow the recipe for fried meatballs. When meatballs are ready, add them to the prepared tomato sauce and simmer for 15-20 minutes over medium heat until liquid is absorbed and meatballs are well-coated with the sauce. Serve with mashed potatoes or rice.

Tomato Sauce

3 tomatoes peeled and chopped
1 onion finely chopped
2 cloves garlic finely chopped
1/2 cup oil
1 bay leaf
Fresh basil, dill or mint
Salt and pepper to taste
Dash of sugar

Sauté onions and garlic in oil. Add chopped tomatoes and other ingredients. Let cook for 20-30 minutes. For a thicker sauce, add more tomato sauce.

EGGPLANT CASSEROLE (MOUSSAKA)

Makes 12 servings

2 large eggplants or 3 medium-size ones
2 pounds hamburger
4 ounces tomato sauce
1 small onion chopped
4 tablespoons chopped parsley
1 tablespoon oregano
1/2 teaspoon cinnamon
Onion or garlic salt to taste
Salt to taste
Oil for frying eggplants

Sauce
4 cups milk
4-6 tablespoons flour for every cup of milk
4-6 ounces cheddar cheese
4 tablespoons butter or margarine
2 eggs

Cut eggplants into 1/2-inch slices. Fry in oil until very well done. They have to be soft. Place on paper towels and press until extra oil is absorbed. Salt while warm. Then, set them aside while preparing the meat filling.

Brown the onion. Add the hamburger. Discard the extra fat. Add the parsley, tomato sauce and

seasoning. Let it cook for five minutes until the ingredients are well-mixed.

Prepare sauce. In a pan, dissolve the butter. Slowly add the flour while mixing with a whisk. Add the milk. Continue mixing. When the sauce is thick, beat the eggs and pour them into the mixture. Cut the cheese in one-inch cubes and add to the sauce.

Use a 9 x 13-inch baking pan. Arrange eggplant slices so that they completely cover the bottom of the pan. Pour the meat filling over eggplants. Place remaining eggplants on top of the filling. Pour the sauce on top. You may wish to sprinkle with bread crumbs. Bake at 350° for one hour or until top is golden brown. Moussaka can be served hot or cold.

I learned a little secret from my cousin. Eggplants absorb too much oil. In frying, you can use half the oil if you flour each slice, quickly dip it in water and then fry it. The flour coating reduces oil absorption.

GROUND MEAT

CABBAGE ROLLS (LAHANODOLMADES)

Makes 10-12 rolls

Use the tender, curved leaves of a green cabbage. Select a cabbage with not too tightly closed leaves. Greek cabbage tends to grow looser.

1 small cabbage
1 small onion minced
6-8 ounces ground meat
3/4 cup rice
1/2 cup oil
1/2 cup parsley minced
Salt and pepper to taste

Egg-lemon sauce
2-3 eggs
Juice of 2 lemons

Bring a large pot of water to boil and add 2 teaspoons of salt. Lower the cabbage into the boiling water. Boil it for 10 minutes until the leaves are wilted and tender. Dip the cooked cabbage into a bowl of cold water to stop the cooking. Peel leaves one by one, trimming any tough stems and the core. Set leaves aside while preparing the stuffing. If the inner leaves are hard to remove, repeat the boiling process.

In Corfu we call cabbage rolls Yaprakia and they are one of my favorite dishes.

In a skillet, sauté the onions in oil until soft (about 5 minutes). Add the meat and sauté

another 5 minutes. Drain the fat. Remove from heat and add the rice, parsley and seasoning.

Reserve some leaves and stems to form a layer at the bottom of a large pan. Lay cabbage leaves flat and place 1-2 tablespoons of the meat and rice mixture in the middle of them. Fold the top over the filling. Continue to fold the sides and roll up the leaves to form tight packets. Place the stuffed leaves in the pan, seam down, and arrange them close together. Make layers of packets and on top of them place a heavy, heat-proof plate. Add enough water to cover the cabbage packets and add the oil. Simmer covered over medium heat for 30-45 minutes or until the rice is cooked and the leaves are tender. Add more water if needed.

Preparation of the Egg-Lemon Sauce

Beat the eggs until frothy. Add the lemon juice and continue beating. Slowly add 2 cups of the cooking liquid into the egg mixture in order to equalize the temperature. If you don't have 2 cups of liquid, you can add chicken stock.

Pour the egg-lemon mixture into the saucepan, and cook it over a very low heat until the sauce thickens, shaking the pan constantly.

In my household, we make the egg-lemon sauce separately and then pour it over the cabbage rolls in the serving dish. Serve hot or cold.

The Zucchini Story

When returning to the United States, I usually spent some time in Athens with my aunt Lena, a first cousin of Mother and the only one left of a family of seven brothers and sisters.

I wanted to be part of the family and remember the good old times. Lena was very helpful in reminding me of certain incidents that I had forgotten.

> "From there on it was zucchini for lunch, zucchini for supper, even zucchini for breakfast."

As a good Greek hostess she wanted to be hospitable and satisfy every little request I had. One day she asked me what I would like to eat. I made the mistake of saying stuffed zucchini, a dish I had not eaten for many years.

As Lena was not cooking for herself, she asked a friend to make a huge bowl of stuffed zucchini with a very tasty egg-lemon sauce. Later I found that she paid the lady to cook the dish and deliver it the next day, warm from the range.

From there on it was zucchini for lunch, zucchini for supper, even zucchini for breakfast. I adored the dish but I felt that zucchinis were coming out of my ears.

There was a ritual attached to the meal. The huge bowl was put in the middle of the table and Lena would say, "Eat. This was made especially for you. Eat. You have to finish it." She never ate the zucchini but she got lots of pleasure seeing me eat one piece after another, scooping the sauce with bread.

The last day before leaving, I had breakfast with my aunt. The remaining two stuffed zucchini were prominently displayed on the table. Nothing was said but I knew what my aunt wanted. She wanted me to finish the dish. I purposely ignored it, drinking my coffee and eating my toast. Finally, it was time to go. "Eat it," I said while I was kissing my aunt goodbye.

P.S. After Lena died, the torch was passed to my cousin. So when I visit her, there is a bowl of stuffed zucchini waiting for me. It is my destiny not to escape the zucchini.

STUFFED ZUCCHINI WITH EGG-LEMON SAUCE

Makes 2-3 servings

4 pounds medium-sized zucchini (3-4)
6-8 ounces ground meat
1 small onion minced
3/4 cup rice
1/2 cup oil
1/2 cup parsley minced
Salt and pepper to taste

Egg-lemon Sauce
3 eggs slightly beaten
Juice of 1 or 2 lemons

Wash zucchini, cut off the ends, and scoop out the insides with a spoon. If the zucchini are too long, cut them to fit your pan. Sauté onion in the oil for 5 minutes. Add the ground meat and the parsley and continue cooking for 5 minutes. Turn the heat off and add the rice to the meat. Stuff the zucchini with the mixture. Place side by side in a pan and add just enough water to barely cover them. Add the oil. Cook for 40 minutes over low heat. In a bowl, beat the eggs with the lemon juice until they are frothy. Slowly add some of the zucchini cooking liquid while beating. Then pour the liquid over the zucchini. Rock the pan gently so that the sauce becomes evenly distributed and starts to thicken. Turn off the heat. Do not overcook. Serve hot or warm.

MEATLOAF (ROLO)

Makes 4-6 servings

2 pounds hamburger
2 eggs
2 slices of French bread (dry)
1/2 cup minced parsley
1/2 cup onion minced
1 tablespoon oregano
1/4 cup milk
8 ounces tomato sauce
2 tablespoons oil
3 hard-boiled eggs
2 teaspoons garlic salt
Salt and pepper to taste

Optional

1 medium bay leaf crushed
Dash of thyme

Sauté the onion in oil. Add two to four tablespoons of water and cook until tender. Add the tomato sauce and the seasoning. Cook until the mixture becomes a sauce. If too thick, add some water. Dip the two slices of dry bread into the milk and squeeze out the excess liquid. Instead of bread, you can use 1/2 cup of seasoned bread crumbs. I prefer the milk bread because it creates a softer meatloaf.

In a bowl, mix hamburger, eggs, bread and half

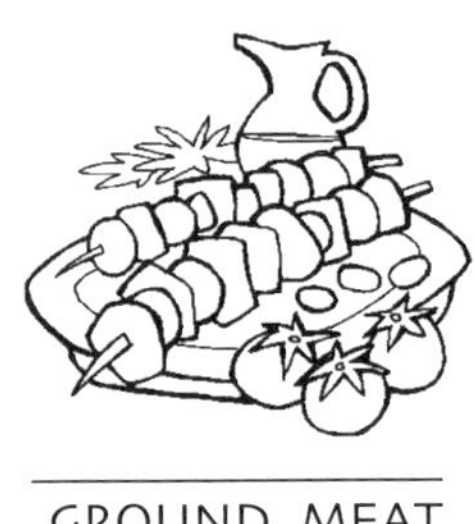

of the sauce. Pat half of the mixture into the bottom of a loaf pan. Shell the hard-boiled eggs and place them along the length of the pan. Now, add the other half of the hamburger mixture and cover the eggs. Cover the top with the remaining tomato sauce.

Bake in a moderate oven for at least one hour until meat is done.

STUFFED GRAPE LEAVES WITH EGG-LEMON SAUCE

For stuffed grape leaves, or dolmades, refer to the recipe on page 22.

To make an egg-lemon sauce, see recipe on page 86. Using the liquid from the pan, combine the egg-lemon sauce with the dolmades liquid and then pour over them. Remove from the burner. Shake the pan from side-to-side. Let stand for ten minutes before serving so that the sauce can thicken.

Serve them as part of a meal with meat, potatoes, or other dishes.

VARIATION: You can make an egg-lemon sauce using the liquid from the pan. If you don't have enough liquid, use some chicken broth. Arrange dolmades on a platter and pour sauce over them.

Poultry & Eggs

Byzantine Church
CORFU, GREECE

POULTRY AND EGGS

We raised poultry for our meat.

I enjoyed working in the poultry house although several times I was chased out by our handsome rooster. At times, I would become attached to a hen and I was always disappointed when she would disappear in due time.

I was assigned to collect the eggs from the nests that I knew about. I learned how to establish a hen in a large basket and select the eggs for hatching. And, I tried to be present when the eggs would hatch and reveal the precious chicks. It was difficult to hold the chicks because they were constantly moving. The mother hen would furiously protect her offspring, attacking anything in sight.

Because chicken was frequently eaten in my household, mother created many ways in which to prepare it. I have included my favorite chicken recipes. Try the one with eggplants. It is unusual and delicious.

POULTRY

EGGS

CHICKEN WITH BÉCHAMEL SAUCE (CHICKEN MILANAISE)

Makes 4-5 servings

2 pounds chicken cut into pieces
One béchamel sauce recipe (See recipe on page 87.)

For Rice

2 cups rice
3/4 to 1 cup frozen peas
1 carrot cut into pieces

Boil the chicken. Remove meat from the bones and set aside.

Cook rice with peas and carrot. Parsley and onion can be added if so desired.

Make béchamel sauce from recipe on page 87. Mix part of the sauce with the cooked rice. Put rice in a ring-shaped mold and reverse it onto a serving dish. The mold has to allow enough space in the center for the boiled chicken pieces. Pour the remainder of the sauce over the chicken and serve.

Mother always referred to this recipe as Chicken Milanaise. It reminds me of an Italian risotto served with chicken pieces and covered with béchamel sauce.

You can use an egg-lemon sauce instead of béchamel sauce.

CHICKEN WITH EGGPLANT

Makes 4-5 servings

2 pounds chicken cut into pieces
1 onion sliced
4 ounces tomato sauce (half of an 8-ounce can)
1 medium eggplant
1 1/2 - 2 cups of water
4-6 tablespoons of oil

In a skillet, brown the chicken on both sides with two tablespoons of oil. Let the chicken absorb the oil. Remove from skillet and set aside. In the same pan, sauté onions for 5-8 minutes with two more tablespoons of oil. Add tomato sauce diluted in water. Let simmer for a few minutes. Cut eggplant into 1/2-inch cubes. Add them to the sauce with the remaining oil. Cover and let simmer for 15-20 minutes until eggplants are soft and they start absorbing the liquid. Add the chicken and the remaining water and simmer for 45 minutes to one hour until the chicken is done and the liquid is absorbed. You might have to stir it a couple of times. Serve with mashed potatoes or the pasta of your choice.

Eggplants tend to produce water in cooking. I suggest that you add water a little at a time. I am giving you a range of oil quantity. The larger the eggplant, the more oil it will absorb.

CHICKEN KAPAMA

Makes 4-5 servings

2 - 3 pound chicken
1 1/2 cups canned tomatoes
2 tablespoons tomato paste
1 teaspoon cinnamon
1/4 teaspoon cloves
3-5 tablespoons oil
Juice of 1 lemon
Salt and pepper to taste
2 cups water

Wash and cut chicken into pieces. Mix the spices and seasoning with the lemon juice and brush onto each piece of chicken, covering them thoroughly. Brown chicken in oil on all sides. Add tomatoes, tomato paste and water. Cook for one hour or more until the chicken is done and liquid is absorbed. If needed, use a little more water.

Serve with mashed potatoes, rice or spaghetti.

The Turkey Story

I don't have a particular recipe for turkey, which in my house was roasted and sometimes stuffed. A recipe of your choice can be found in a regular cookbook.

In Greece, turkey is usually cooked for Christmas and lamb is the traditional meal for Easter.

Just seeing the word turkey reminds me of a bizarre adventure I had as a child. I was a twelve-year-old "little miss" concerned with my appearance and proper manners.

At that time, I was using my bicycle to go to and from school, which was located at the center of town and about two miles from my home. There were no school buses or corresponding public transportation. On rainy days, I would walk to school with my umbrella and raincoat. Frequently after school, I would stop by my father's office to see if he had any errands for me. Father would oftentimes load my bicycle down with groceries. I remember that once I had to carry a broom.

"...someone had given my father a live turkey. He asked me to take the bird home on my bicycle."

It was two or three days before Christmas and someone had given my father a live turkey. He asked me to take the bird home on my bicycle. After we tied the turkey's legs together and put him in a canvas bag that we hung on the bicycle, I mounted the two-wheeler. After I made my first turn onto a very busy street, the bird began flapping his wings vigorously, the bag opened up and the critter went flying out into the street. I stopped the bicycle, left it at the side of the street and began the chase. The longer I pursued the turkey, the further away he got, flapping his wings all the while. How embarrassing it was for a cute little miss, who was trying to establish herself in society, to be chasing a bird down the street!

The flying turkey passed the butcher shop, then the cobbler shop and continued on past a bookstore and a pastry shop. Finally, he lost his energy in front of the quilt shop. The quilt-maker, who was acquainted with me and my father, rushed out of the shop shouting, "Leave it to me!" With his long legs and physical agility, he was able to catch the bird with little effort. "How far do you have to go?" asked the quilt-maker. "Two miles," I answered. "Then we had better tie his wings together so there won't be another escape." The helpful man tied the wings and put the turkey back into the sack hanging from my bicycle. Frazzled and exhausted, I mounted my bike and rode home slowly. I was driving with one hand on the bars and other hand on the bird.

That was the first and last turkey I ever transported for my father.

CHICKEN WITH PEPPERS AND BLACK OLIVES

Makes 4-5 servings

2 pounds chicken
6-8 tablespoons oil
1 medium onion chopped
4 large green bell peppers sliced
4 ounces black olives sliced
Juice of 2 lemons

Brown chicken on both sides in half the oil. Add lemon juice and let cook for 10 minutes so that chicken absorbs the taste of the lemon. Remove from pan and put it aside. In same saucepan, add the rest of the oil. Sauté the onion for 5 minutes or more. Add the peppers and cook for 10 minutes until they wilt. Add chicken and olives and let cook for one hour on medium heat or until liquid is absorbed. Peppers will produce lots of liquid that needs to be absorbed so that the taste is not lost.

This is a good recipe to use when there are too many peppers in your garden.

CHICKEN IN TOMATO SAUCE

Makes 4 - 5 servings

2 - 2 1/2 pounds of chicken skinned and cut into pieces
1 medium onion finely chopped
2 cloves of garlic finely chopped
1 large green pepper sliced
1 can stewed tomatoes
6-8 tablespoons of tomato sauce
4 tablespoons oil
1/2 cup red wine (optional)
Black olives for garnish

For seasoning

Salt and pepper to taste
1 teaspoon oregano
1 teaspoon rosemary
1 bay leaf

Brown the chicken on both sides in half the oil. Season with salt and pepper. Remove from pan and put it aside. In the same pan, add the remaining oil and sauté the garlic and onions with the oregano, rosemary and bay leaf. Cook for 10 minutes until onions are golden brown. Then add the green pepper, the wine, the stewed tomatoes and tomato sauce and cook for 5-10 minutes. Reduce heat. Add chicken.

Cover and let it cook for one hour, turning over the chicken a few times. Make sure the liquid is absorbed and the sauce is thick. Garnish with olives and serve.

CHICKEN WITH OREGANO (CHICKEN RIGANATO)

Makes 4-6 servings

2 - 3 pounds of chicken cut into pieces
2 tablespoons oil
3/4 to 1 cup water
Juice of 2 lemons
2 tablespoons of oregano
Salt and pepper to taste

Heat the oil in a skillet. Add the chicken and brown on all sides. If needed, add a little more oil. I try to keep oil to a minimum. Add water, the juice of one lemon, salt, pepper and oregano. Bring the water to a boil. Cook for about half an hour. Lower the heat. Add the juice of another lemon and any additional seasoning you desire. Cook until chicken is tender and the liquid is absorbed. You might have to turn the chicken pieces a few times.

CHICKEN WITH OKRA

Makes 4-5 servings

2 pounds chicken cut into pieces
1 pound okra fresh or frozen
4 tablespoons oil
4 ounces tomato sauce (half can)
1 can stewed tomatoes (14-16 ounces)
1 cup water or less
Onion - optional

To eliminate the slimy surface of the okra, soak the vegetable in a water and vinegar mixture. For one pound of okra, use one-half cup of vinegar and water to cover. Let stand for 30 minutes and then dispose of the liquid.

Brown the chicken on all sides. Add okra, tomato sauce, tomatoes and water. Let simmer for 40-60 minutes. Turn the chicken pieces a few times. I also like to add one half of a sliced onion. Serve with potatoes of your choice.

POACHED EGGS (EGGS BAGNO MARIA)

Makes 1-2 servings

2 eggs
1 tablespoon oil
Salt and pepper to taste
Juice of 1 lemon
Water

Pour one to two inches of water into a shallow skillet. When it comes to a boil, add one tablespoon oil. Reduce the heat. Break the eggs and add them to the water. Add the seasoning on top of the eggs. Before removing eggs from the water, add the lemon juice and let it cook with the eggs for one to two minutes.

Aunt Maro

I clearly remember Aunt Maro. Her name was Tante Maro in French. She was my mother's first cousin. When the Italian bombardments of Corfu Island became frequent and unpredictable, Tante Maro and her daughter, Sia, moved in with us.

"Then, she would perform a little dance as she brought the skillet to the table and serve us large amounts of the nutritious but undesirable food."

We had a bomb shelter for protection, although I doubt it would have protected us from a direct hit.

Tante Maro was a slightly-built, petite woman with a tremendous amount of energy. She reminded me of a little bee fluttering from flower to flower. After moving in with us, she took over many of the household activities. Maro moved quickly and efficiently from one project to another, leaving everyone else behind. She would cook and clean, wash dishes, cultivate and harvest the garden, and feed the animals.

She always prepared nutritious meals for the younger people. We were the new generation and we had to be well-fed. We never went without food. I still bless our mothers who sacrificed so many of their needs to give us the best of everything - food and clothes.

Tante Maro had a specialty that she would encourage us to eat. Every week we would slaughter a rooster or a rabbit and would save the liver, cut it into small pieces and sauté it in oil. Maro would then add a couple of eggs and scramble it all together.

Liver was not the young people's favorite food. In order to entice us into eating it, she would serve the meal on an old table we had in the garden. It was among the flowers and placed under the shade of the almond tree. My aunt would cover it with a fancy linen tablecloth, two beautifully hand-painted plates, fine silverware and lace napkins that would be tied around our necks. Then, she would perform a little dance as she brought the skillet to the table and serve us large amounts of the nutritious but undesirable food.

After serving the food, she would taste a bit and exclaim how delicious it tasted and how good it was for us. We did not agree. We ate the eggs and threw the liver, piece by piece, on the ground. That continued for some time until the cats began to congregate under the table and catch the morsels of liver in mid-air. Those darn cats gave us away. Eventually, my aunt served us in the kitchen; smaller portions several times a week.

EGGS WITH LIVER

Servings depend on quantity of eggs and liver

Liver (from rabbit or chicken)
Oil
Eggs to scramble
Seasoning

Cut livers into small pieces. Sauté in oil. Season with salt and pepper to taste. Beat eggs. Add them to livers and scramble until done.

POACHED EGGS IN TOMATO SAUCE

Makes 2-4 servings

4 tablespoons oil
4-5 tablespoons tomato sauce
1 large pepper chopped
1 small onion chopped
1 large tomato chopped
Salt and pepper to taste
2-4 eggs

In a skillet, sauté onion in the oil. Add the pepper. Cook 5-10 minutes until ingredients are tender. Add the tomato, cut in small pieces, and the tomato sauce. Let the sauce cook until thick.

Break 2-4 eggs and add to the sauce. Cover skillet and let eggs cook until done.

SCRAMBLED EGGS IN TOMATO SAUCE (STRAPATSO)

This recipe is popular in Corfu, my island. Make the same basic sauce as for the poached eggs above, but scramble the eggs in the sauce. It's necessary to stir the eggs in the sauce several times.

Seafood & Snails

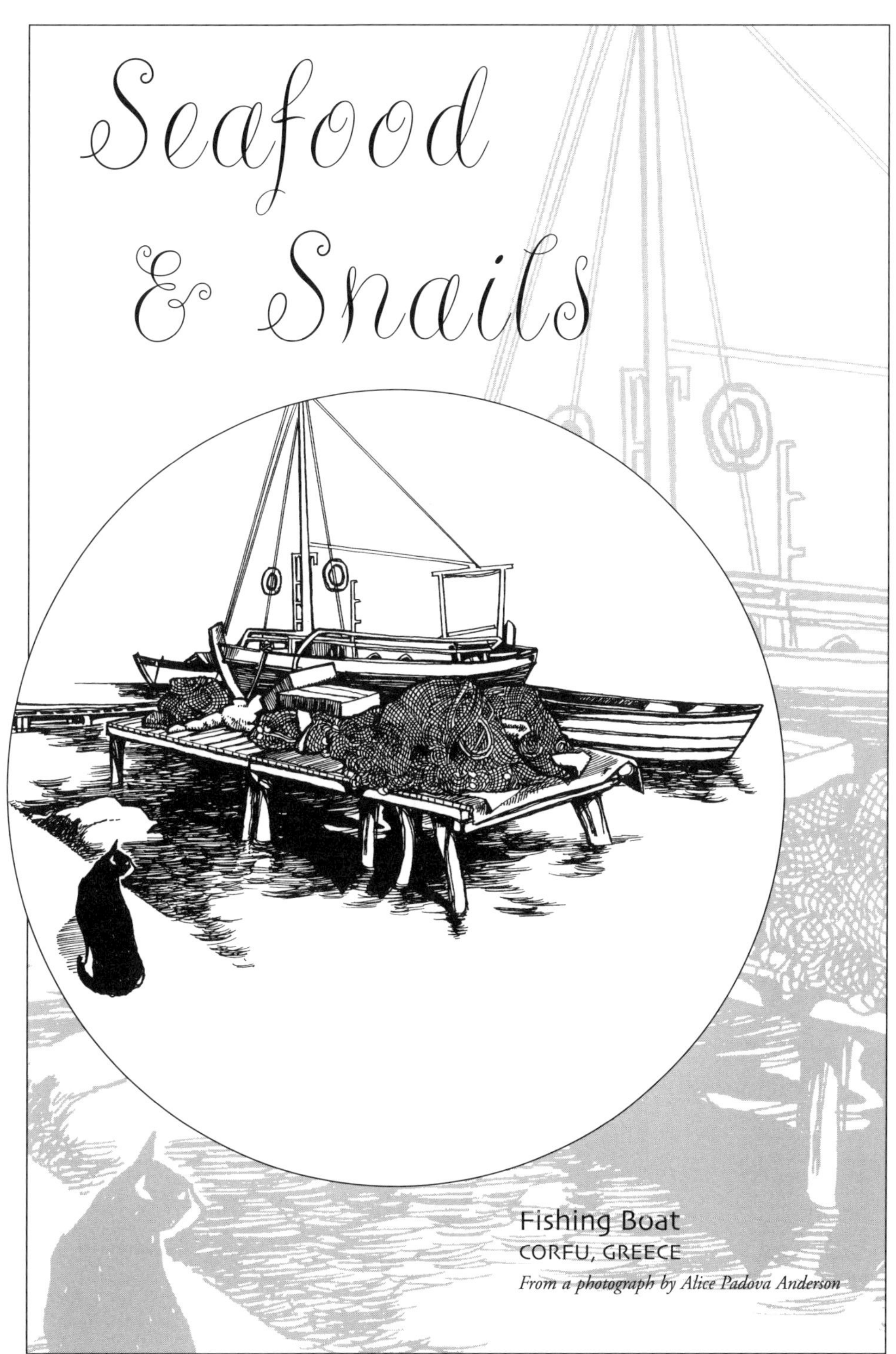

Fishing Boat
CORFU, GREECE
From a photograph by Alice Padova Anderson

SEAFOOD - SNAILS

Greece has miles of coastline and hundreds of islands. It is a paradise for the professional and amateur fisherman. Fish is prepared as simply as possible. Small fish are floured, fried, and eaten whole. Other fish are poached, broiled, grilled, baked or made into soups and stews. Octopus, calamari and cuttlefish, often cooked with rice or pasta, are very popular and usually served in fish restaurants as appetizers.

The secret to good fish is freshness. You have to go to the market early in the morning when fishermen bring in their catch. Growing up in Corfu, I lived in a neighborhood with many fishermen. I remember them going through the streets of the neighborhood advertising their fish. They would carry a hand scale and weigh the fresh fish in front of the customer.

Although frozen fish, local or imported, have been introduced into the market, Greeks, especially islanders, love the taste of a fresh salt water fish.

FISH BIANCO

Makes 6-8 servings

2 pounds white fish

2 stalks celery chopped

2 medium potatoes cut in round slices

2 small onions sliced

2-4 cloves of garlic minced

1/2 cup oil

Water

Juice of one lemon

Salt and pepper to taste

Sauté onions and garlic in oil. Add the sliced potatoes, celery and water to cover and let them boil for 10 minutes. Add the fish cut in portions and more water if needed. Cover the pan and let the stew boil on slow heat. When the liquid is absorbed, add the lemon juice and serve in a soup plate.

Bianco means white in Italian. My Italian friend, Ann, told me that bianco is a term that means nothing has been added to the dish to change its color.

FISH PLAKI

Makes 3-4 servings

1 pound fish fillets (cod or other)
1 large onion sliced
4 garlic cloves minced
2 green onions diced
2 stalks celery diced
1/2 cup parsley minced
3 tomatoes sliced
1/2 cup oil
2 tablespoons oregano
1 bay leaf
Lemon juice of 1 or 2 lemons
Salt and pepper to taste

Sauté garlic and onions in oil until soft. Add celery, parsley, tomatoes and bay leaf. Season to taste. Simmer for 15-30 minutes until it reaches the consistency of a sauce. Place the fish fillets in the sauce. Add the oregano and lemon juice. Simmer for another 30 minutes until fish is done.

Baking method
Prepare the sauce. Place fish in a greased baking pan. Sprinkle with oregano. Cover with the sauce. Add lemon juice. Sprinkle with breadcrumbs (optional). Bake at 350° for 30-45 minutes until fish is done.

Fishing Story

During the occupation, we depended upon food from the bountiful sea. We had a row boat. Her name was Aliki or Alice in English. Father was very proud of Aliki. He would paint and repair her, and put her on shore during the winter and bad weather.

During the summer he would construct a tent, a straight piece of cloth which scarcely protected us from the sun, on the boat. We would also use Aliki to go swimming a couple of miles away on a remote but beautiful deserted beach. We women folk learned how to row and guide the boat safely in rocky areas of the sea and designated places of disembarkment. There were no jetties or steps available at that time. Sometimes we had to get wet in order to reach the shore. But we always seemed to manage. Writing this story reminds me of the wonderful times we had with that boat.

"For the men, fishing was a bonding experience and an excellent opportunity for storytelling."

I still know how to row using both oars; putting them in at the proper angle and lowering them into the sea so that they can pull more water. And, I still know how to turn the boat around by rowing each oar in the opposite direction.

But, Aliki was mainly used for fishing. Fish supplemented our daily diets and provided entertainment in our lives. Mother was quite a fisherwoman. She would frequently return from a fishing trip with her baskets full and put the men to shame. Although fishing was a family affair, the men had their deep sea expeditions. Michael, George and Father, all good neighbors and friends, would go fishing in spots where they knew the currents and the fish unique to that area. During the summer months and the fishing season, the expeditions occurred several times a week. The men would catch all sizes of fish. The larger ones we would boil, bake or broil. The smaller ones we would fry or use in my mother's locally famous bouillabaisse. Her recipe is in this book.

For the men, fishing was a bonding experience and an excellent opportunity for storytelling. Some of the stories I didn't believe, but the following one sounded credible.

The men had developed certain routines on their fishing ventures which they repeated with every trip. One of the rituals was to throw the anchor once they arrived at the designated spot, and then shout, "Bottom."

One day, Michael was in charge. He stepped onto the bow, hoisted the heavy iron anchor and, in a very theatrical manner, threw it as far out as he could. "Bottom," he shouted. And to the bottom it went, never to be recovered. Someone had forgotten to tie the anchor rope to the boat. That day, the three fishermen returned home with empty baskets.

FRIED COD

Makes 4-6 servings

2 pounds dried cod
Frying oil
Bread crumbs
Salt and pepper to taste

Cut the dried cod into portions. Soak in water for 24 hours, changing it 2-3 times. Drain. Remove the skin and bones. Coat the fish in crumbs and fry in a deep pan of very hot oil until done.

VARIATION: Make a thick batter of flour and water. Add a little baking soda and oil. Dip the fish in the batter and fry.

Traditionally fried cod is served with garlic sauce (see Skordalia on page 84).

SEAFOOD & SNAILS

MOTHER'S BOUILLABAISSE

Makes 6-8 servings

This recipe is very similar to the soup, Kakavia, prepared on many Greek islands by the fishermen who stay at sea for several days. They cook the catch of the day in a large kettle called a kakavi. Because there were fishermen in my family, we made this soup several times. It consists of small fish cooked with vegetables.

2 pounds small fish of different varieties

2 onions chopped

2 medium potatoes cut in pieces

2 celery stalks with their leaves

1/2 cup or more of oil

Salt and pepper to taste

2-3 medium tomatoes (optional)

Juice of 2 lemons

Use a large pan with enough water to cover the potatoes, onions, tomatoes and oil and bring to a boil. Let them boil for 10 minutes. Add the celery, the seasoning and the fish. Boil until the fish separates from the bones.

Serve hot with lemon juice and bread. Fish bones and heads are not removed. This soup is very nutritious and tasty. And, it is an acquired taste.

When mother had the time, she would pass the soup through a food mill and serve it smooth and thick.

OCTOPUS PILAF

Makes 4-6 servings

1 small octopus
1 onion chopped
1/2 cup oil
1 tablespoon tomato paste
2 large ripe tomatoes
1 cup rice
Salt and pepper to taste

In order to tenderize the octopus, cook it for 30 minutes in seawater or salted water. Drain and cut into small pieces. Sauté onions. Add the pieces of octopus and cook for 5-10 minutes. Add the chopped and skinned tomatoes and the tomato paste diluted in water. Cover the pot and cook until tender.

The octopus can be served over pilaf or add the rice in the pan and cook it with the octopus. If you want to cook it this way, make sure you add enough liquid to make 2 or 2 1/2 cups of liquid. Add the rice and cook covered for 20 minutes over a low heat.

Remove from heat and let it cool for 5-10 minutes. Then serve.

OCTOPUS OR SQUID PASTITSADA

Makes 4-6 servings

2 pounds octopus or squid
2 pounds tomatoes cut into pieces
1 cup oil
2 tablespoons tomato paste diluted in water
2 chopped onions
2-3 bay leaves
1 teaspoon cinnamon
2-3 whole cloves
Salt and pepper to taste

Cook the octopus in seawater or salted water for at least 30 minutes. Remove from water and cut it into pieces. Sauté onions in the oil. Add tomatoes, tomato paste and seasonings to the octopus. Cook over a moderate heat for 40 minutes to an hour until tender and liquid is absorbed. It makes a thick sauce that can be used with macaroni and other pastas.

PILAF WITH MUSSELS

Makes 4-6 servings

2 dozen mussels
1 onion chopped
1/2 cup oil
1/2 cup dry white wine
2 tablespoons tomato paste diluted in water
1 cup rice
2 cups water
1/4 cup chopped parsley
Salt and pepper to taste

Remove mussels from shell. Clean and strain.

Sauté onion in oil. Dissolve tomato paste in some water. Add it to the mussels and simmer for a few minutes. Add the remaining water, onion, oil and rice. Bring to a boil. Reduce heat. Add wine. Cover and simmer for 20 minutes. Remove from heat. Set it aside for 5-10 minutes for the liquids to be absorbed. Then serve.

I find that rice absorbs the wonderful flavors of seafood. Every spoonful of rice smells and tastes like seafood.

In my family we have used oysters, clams and other kinds of seafood found in Greece. The recipe is the same and the dish is delicious.

SEA URCHINS

Sea urchins are part of a fisherman's diet and considered a delicacy. When harvested at the proper time, during the full moon in the summer months, they provide their delicate clusters of orange eggs that are attached to the shell.

To open a sea urchin, use a sharp-pointed knife and cut a large hole in the flat top of the urchin. Special scissors are now available for better efficiency.

Urchins can be served in the shell with a squeeze of lemon. But make sure that the inside is clean and the eggs are exposed.

I once asked my friend Angelo, an experienced fisherman, if there were male and female urchins. He said that he didn't know. He only knew of full and not-full urchins.

During the summer months, I have made many sea dives to retrieve sea urchins for my family. At times, I have been successful and discovered urchins full of eggs. At other times, I have been unsuccessful and only found barren ones that we discarded.

When diving in the sea among the black algae in order to harvest the urchins, I look for the ones that are plump. They have shorter spines and a purplish color on their tops. They are the ones with the eggs. The urchins with long spines have no eggs.

SMOKED HERRING (RENGA)

1 herring
Oil
Lemon juice

Wrap the herring in foil and set it on an electric burner for about 5-8 minutes on each side. This procedure will loosen the skin which can then be easily peeled off.

Cut the herring into small pieces. Pour oil and lemon juice over them.

Renga frequently accompanies legume soups made with lentils or other types of beans.

Smoked herring is a popular appetizer throughout Greece.

SNAILS

If it rained at night, the next day would be a good one for picking snails. After a heavy rain, snails would come out all over the garden. They could be found on leafy shrubs, crawling on the trunks of trees, and in wall crevices that encircled our property. They were small, medium and large.

We didn't cook them very often because it required a long and tedious procedure to prepare them. But they were delicious. Not many people know how to prepare them and others don't want to fool with them. I have prepared them a couple of times, but no one cooks them better than our neighbor, Spyridoula.

PREPARING AND COOKING SNAILS

Gather snails in a bowl or saucepan. Cover container with lid and put weight on it so that the snails won't escape. Keep them enclosed 3-4 days and feed them greens, such as lettuce leaves. Greens will clean their digestive systems. Remove any dirt they produce. After cleaning the snails, wash them in salted water. Change the water 2-3 times. Put them in salty water and boil for 15 minutes. Then, with a slotted spoon, remove them from the water. For better cleaning, use a sharp knife to open a small hole in the back of the shell and rinse them in the water in which they were cooked so they will maintain a salty taste.

Sauté one chopped onion and two chopped garlic cloves. Add one to two pounds of spinach, depending on how many snails are available. Let the spinach wilt. Add oil and two grated tomatoes and cook for 10-15 minutes. Add red hot pepper and the snails. Spyridoula would always make the dish so hot it would bring tears to your eyes. Let them cook for another 15-20 minutes until the liquid is absorbed and then serve. Toothpicks will be needed to pull out the snails.

Add more tomatoes and oil if a thicker sauce is desirable. Use your judgment on the amount of pepper. The sauce might need more water.

The Snail Story

Early in my life, probably at the age of three, my parents decided that I should learn the value of work. They thought that something that I liked to do would be a good project for me.

Garden snails were always an attraction to me. Because they were slow-moving, I could catch them easily. They would hide in obscure places that only I knew. Discovering them had a special appeal to me.

"You like snails," father said one day. "You gather them and I will pay you. Then you can buy the colorful yarns you need to finish the embroidery on your seat cushion. I will pay you a lepto (less than one penny) for every large snail you catch and half a lepto for each of the smaller ones." Sure enough, the next day I went out early in the morning and gathered snails and put them in a bowl and covered it with a lid. Mother placed a weight on top of the lid so the slimy critters could not escape. Around one o'clock I went to the garden and waited for father to come home. Mother supervised closely from the window above. I lined up my snails according to size in two parallel lines. One line was for the large ones and the other one was for the small ones. But the lines would keep changing as the snails moved. When father arrived home on his bicycle I proudly showed him my catch. "Now," he said, "let's count them." With my limited knowledge of numbers, I counted fifteen large ones, skipping a few numbers along the way. "Wait," said father. "I don't think you have that many large ones." But I argued that they were big enough for me.

"You like snails," father said one day. "You gather them and I will pay you."

"But they are not big enough for me!" exclaimed father. "Put a couple of them in the other line. They all have to be the same size." Reluctantly, I moved a few large snails to the other line. "Not enough," said father. "You can only keep ten in the first line. Don't forget that I am paying according to size." After arguing back and forth, we settled on the numbers and the amount of money. It took me a couple of snail days to make enough money to buy the yarn and a small purse in which to keep it.

SEAFOOD & SNAILS

BAKED SARDINES

2 pounds sardines
4-6 cloves of garlic minced
2 or more tomatoes sliced
1/2 cup oil
Oregano and thyme in combination or separate
Parsley for decoration

Wash the sardines. Drain. Arrange them in layers in a round baking pan. Add the minced garlic. Pour the oil evenly over the sardines. Sprinkle with oregano or thyme or both. Cut tomatoes in round slices and arrange them on top of the sardines. Bake in moderate oven at 350° until the liquid is well absorbed. The juice from the tomatoes provides most of the liquid for this dish. The flavors blend well together.

We eat cooked sardines whole. However, the fish heads can be removed before or after they have been cooked. Open sardines and remove the bones after cooking, if you so desire.

VARIATION: You can cut potatoes in round slices and put them at the bottom of the pan. Potatoes will absorb some of the juice from the tomatoes and the fish.

This hearty dish was prepared for the first time by our village helper.

SEAFOOD & SNAILS

STEWED FISH WITH ONIONS (BOURTHETO)

You can use white fish and/or cod, haddock or red snapper fillets. In Corfu, we prefer using the fish scorpios and rufios. We cook them whole.

Because of the large quantity of onions, the dish can be heavy. You can lighten this dish by using the following method.

Slice the onions. Put them in a saucepan, add water, and simmer them for ten to fifteen minutes. Throw away the liquid. Then add the oil, sauté them and proceed with the recipe.

3 pounds fish

1/2 cup oil

1 1/2 cup water

2-3 sliced onions (2 cups)

1 teaspoon red pepper

1 teaspoon paprika

Salt to taste

Cut fish into servings. Sauté onions in oil or use the above-described method. Add part of the water and let it simmer for ten to fifteen minutes until onions are soft. Add the fish, the seasoning and the rest of the water. Cook for another 15 minutes until the fish flakes easily with a fork.

Serve with garlic sauce or mashed potatoes.

This hot dish is very popular in Corfu. You can make it as mild or as hot as you wish by varying the amount of pepper.

STIFADO WITH OCTOPUS

Makes 4-6 servings

2 pounds octopus

4-6 cloves of garlic finely chopped

1 pound small onions or slice large ones into quarters

1 pound tomatoes peeled and cut into small pieces (2 medium)

1/2 cup oil

2-4 tablespoons vinegar

2 bay leaves

1 stick cinnamon or 1/2 teaspoon cinnamon

Salt and pepper to taste

1/2 cup red wine (optional)

Cook the octopus for 30 minutes in salt water. Remove water and cut into pieces. Sauté onions and garlic. Add tomatoes and let them cook for 5 minutes. Add the octopus and the other ingredients. Cook on low heat for 1 hour or until octopus is tender and the liquid is absorbed.

Add more water if needed.

Vegetables

The Old Town
CORFU, GREECE

VEGETABLES

Corfu has a great variety of cultivated and wild vegetables. The soil gives them the most wonderful flavor. I always remember how sweet and tender our sweet peas were.

It is common to have a vegetable garden in the back of the house that produces year-round.

Because of the abundance and variety of vegetables, cooks have invented many ways of cooking them from the simple boiling to frying, adding egg-lemon sauce, to making pies to cooking two or three vegetables together.

As we had a large garden when I was growing up, we had vegetables all season. I can remember the eggplants, okra, tomatoes, peppers, zucchini and other vegetables in the summer, and the large cabbage heads and greens in the winter. The artichokes were planted in rows along the side of the garden, while the squash were hanging from the vines. Wild vegetables supplemented the great array of vegetables and could be collected from October to April in the fields and hills of Corfu.

SPINACH RICE (SPANAKORIZO)

Makes 4 - 6 servings

2 packages frozen spinach (10 ounces each)
1/2 cup rice
4-6 tablespoons oil
1/2 onion sliced
1 cup water
1 sprig fresh mint or 1 tablespoon fresh dill
Salt and pepper to taste

Sauté onion in oil. Add the rice and sauté together for one minute. Season with salt, pepper and herbs. Thaw spinach and squeeze out excess water. Add the spinach and one cup of water. Cook covered for 15-20 minutes. Do not mix while cooking. Let the liquid become absorbed. Then mix. Use it to accompany fish or meat. Or, serve it as a main dish with some feta cheese.

OKRA IN TOMATO SAUCE (OKRA YAHNI)

Makes 4 servings

1 pound okra

2 medium onions

3 ripe tomatoes or 1 lb. can of tomatoes

1/3 cup oil

Parsley

Dash of sugar if using fresh tomatoes

Trim the stems off the okra with a knife. Wash pods. Because okra has a gooey substance on the pods, soak the pods in a water and vinegar mixture (1/2 cup vinegar per pound of okra) for 30 minutes. Rinse under cold water and discard the gooey liquid. Drain and dry okra with a paper towel.

Sauté onions. Add tomatoes and parsley and simmer for 5-10 minutes. Meanwhile, place the okra in a saucepan. Pour the sauce over the okra. Add enough water to cover. Simmer over a low heat until okra is tender. Don't stir. You want to keep the okra whole.

EGGPLANTS

In my experience, many people don't like the bitter taste of eggplants. I love it. I grew up with that bitter taste.

In order to get rid of some of the bitterness, slice eggplants, salt their surfaces and place in a colander for one-half hour, or you can slice the eggplant and put the pieces into salt water for 30-60 minutes. Rinse before using in both cases.

I like the bitter taste. I also like the texture of the skin. So, I never use the above-mentioned methods except when my guests ask me to do so.

Many times, I cut the eggplants into cubes, leaving the skins intact, and boil them for 10 to 15 minutes in water and then use them in sauces. This method cuts down the cooking time and eliminates some of the bitter taste without soaking in salt water.

Eggplant adds taste to casseroles and sauces. It quickly absorbs the oil and tomato sauce while adding to the blending of flavors and the consistency of the dish.

FRIED EGGPLANTS AND ZUCCHINI

Cut zucchini lengthwise into strips. Cut eggplants into slices. Fry them in oil. Season when hot and serve as appetizers. Or, put the fried vegetables in a bowl and pour some vinegar over them. Let stand for a few hours, then serve.

Can be used as an appetizer or accompany main dishes of meat and fish.

BAKED EGGPLANTS IN TOMATO SAUCE

Makes 4-6 servings

1 medium eggplant sliced and fried in oil

Sauce

3 cloves of garlic sliced

1/2 onion sliced

1 green pepper sliced

1 can (14-15 ounces) of diced or stewed tomatoes

2 - 4 tablespoons tomato sauce

Salt and pepper to taste

Topping

Parmesan cheese

Breadcrumbs

Slice and fry eggplant in oil. The preparation method described in the Moussaka recipe can be used. For the sauce, sauté the onion and garlic. Add diced tomatoes, tomato sauce and sliced pepper. Arrange the fried eggplant in a baking pan and pour the sauce over it. Top it with cheese and bread crumbs. Bake at 350° for 45 minutes to one hour. If you are using a small pan, make two layers of the eggplant.

VEGETABLES

EGGPLANT WITH PEPPERS CASSEROLE

Makes 6-8 servings

2 medium eggplants cut into 1-inch cubes or into strips
3 medium green bell peppers sliced
3 small onions sliced
1 bunch parsley minced
2 teaspoons oregano
3 tablespoons tomato paste in 1/2 cup water
8 ounces tomato sauce
1/2 - 3/4 cup oil
Salt and pepper to taste

Cut eggplants into cubes or strips. Season them with salt and pepper. Spread them over the bottom of a pan. Slice the peppers and onions. Mix them with the minced parsley and oregano. Spread over top of eggplants. In a pan, mix the tomato paste, water and tomato sauce with the oil and then pour over the vegetables. Bake in a moderate oven for 40 - 50 minutes until tender and the liquid is absorbed.

Use a large pan because the ingredients are bulky before cooking. I place the eggplant on the bottom because they absorb the oil and tomato sauce and become very sweet and tender. I have used 1 cup oil in the past, but I cut down the amount because I think it will be too oily for many people's taste.

I discovered this recipe on a piece of paper in Mother's book. I remembered that she made it a number of times. So, I gave it a try. My house smelled of peppers. And my dinner guests enjoyed the casserole.

Bake at 350° for 1 1/2 - 2 hours until all the ingredients are blended.

This recipe can be served as a main dish with feta cheese. And, it can be served on top of rice, macaroni or polenta.

EGGPLANT PUREE

Makes 4 servings

1 medium eggplant

2 tablespoons oil

1/4 cup warm milk

Salt and pepper to taste

Oil to fry

Fresh parsley to garnish

Cut eggplant into slices and fry (see Moussaka recipe on page 115). Puree in a blender with the milk, the oil, and the seasoning.

BAKED VERSION: Cut eggplant into slices and bake at 350° for 45 minutes until tender. Peel off the skins if you don't like their bitter taste. Mix in a blender with the milk, the oil and the seasoning.

Pureed eggplant has a mild taste and it is a good accompaniment to spicy meats and fish dishes.

STUFFED EGGPLANT (IMAM BAYILDI)

Makes 4-6 servings

6 long slender Asian eggplants (2 pounds)

Salt and pepper to taste

1 cup water

4 tomatoes skinned and chopped or 2 cups crushed canned tomatoes

Stuffing

1 cup olive oil

6 - 12 garlic cloves chopped

1/4 to 1/2 cup chopped parsley

If fresh tomatoes are used, add a pinch of sugar to reduce acidity.

Remove stems from eggplants. Peel 1/2-inch strips of skin lengthwise at intervals to give a striped effect.

To make the stuffing, warm the oil in a saucepan. Sauté the garlic and then add the parsley. Let the mixture cool before using.

BAKED METHOD: In a saucepan, sauté eggplants until tender and soft on all sides. Transfer eggplants into a baking dish. Cut a lengthwise slit through the side of each eggplant, being careful not to split the eggplant. Open the slit to make a pocket. Stuff each eggplant with the garlic-parsley mixture. Arrange the eggplants side by

This dish originated in Turkey.

side in the baking dish. Pour the remaining stuffing and tomatoes over the top. Bake at 350° for 40-45 minutes until the liquid is absorbed and eggplants are very soft. You might need to add some additional water. Serve cold.

TOP OF THE STOVE METHOD: Follow the same procedure for preparing eggplants as for the baked eggplant. Arrange the stuffed eggplants in a saucepan. Add the remaining ingredients and water. Cook over a medium heat until eggplants are soft and tender, and the liquid is absorbed (40-45 minutes). You may need to add some more water. Stir occasionally to avoid burning. Eggplants scorch easily. You may want to lower the heat. Serve cold as a main dish.

If Asian eggplants aren't available, use the globe variety (2 medium eggplants). Cut them in half lengthwise and sauté them. Make the slit for stuffing on the cut side and put that side down in the pan.

I remember my mother using uncooked pieces of garlic and parsley to stuff the eggplant pockets instead of the stuffing mixture.

Use less garlic if it is too strong for you.

Use less oil if desired. Less oil will affect the taste.

I was told that this recipe came about when an imam's wife surprised her husband with a new dish. When the imam ate the food, he was so satisfied that he fainted.

Another version of the story is that the imam fainted when he discovered the meal floating in oil because olive oil was expensive.

ABOUT TSIGARELI

There is an art in selecting and combining wild greens for tsigareli, one which I have not mastered.

Our household helper, a village woman with expertise in cooking village dishes, thought that I had no idea how to properly gather greens. One day, she sent her husband and me to the village to collect greens. I was so excited to learn some of the names and shapes of the greens that I over-harvested. The two of us, armed with a sharp knife, cut the luscious greens to the ground and picked several leaves from the ones that had started to go to seed.

After one hour of intensive gathering, we managed to fill four plastic bags with greens. Feeling very proud, we brought them home and discovered that half of them were discarded by the helper because they were "no good." They did not pass her inspection. We learned that they were of inferior quality. They were not the right combination or harvested in the right proportion.

I humbled myself before the chef and let her teach me a lesson. I told her that the next time, she was coming along and that I intended to write down the names of the plants, take photographs and document the great variety of greens on the island.

I use greens myself, but I learned that my knowledge and experience did not match that of the village expert.

TSIGARELI (OR TSIGARI)

Makes 4 servings

2 pounds greens or wild greens

2 medium onions diced

1/2 to 2/3 cup oil

1 can tomato sauce (8 ounces)

1 cup water

Hot pepper and salt to taste

In a deep skillet, sauté the onions in some of the oil. Sauté the greens, stirring them until they wilt. Add the water, tomato sauce, remaining oil, pepper and salt. Let them simmer until water is absorbed.

Serve it as a side dish.

This is a Corfu peasant dish. It can be made hot or mild, depending on the amount of pepper you use. Village people like it hot.

We generally use wild greens collected from the hills and the valleys of Corfu. The variety is endless and plentiful. A combination of wild greens with other greens like spinach or Swiss chard work nicely together. Use some bitter greens such as dandelions and mustard greens. You can also add chopped parsley, chopped green onions or substitute leeks for onions. Use your imagination.

Diced canned tomatoes (16 ounce can) or 2 to 3 fresh tomatoes can be used as a substitute.

Tsigari - a Greek term meaning sauté.

Dalia

When growing up, I had a very good friend named Dalia. We came from the same neighborhood and we both attended the same elementary school. Often we would walk to school together. Dalia was a very spirited girl, full of energy and mischief. Her mischief was the innocent kind.

One afternoon, when Mother and Father had to be out of the house, they invited Dalia to keep me company. Grandfather and Grandmother were in their bedrooms napping. To keep the two of us busy, mother gave us potatoes to peel for supper.

"Why don't we throw a potato down the stairs," she said, "and see what happens?"

We started peeling, but found it very boring. Then Dalia had a bright idea. "Why don't we throw a potato down the stairs," she said, "and see what happens?" In my family's home, there was a very long staircase from the third floor down to the second. We released one potato which, after numerous bumps, landed at the bottom of the stairs. I went down to pick it up, brought it back up and released it again. This time it took a different path. It skipped a couple of steps but landed safely. "It would be fun to release two potatoes at the same time," Dalia said. So, I took one potato, she took another one and we pushed them down the stairs together. Each potato performed a different dance. What we were doing was exciting to us.

"Why don't we throw more at one time," suggested Dalia. So, we took a bucket full of potatoes and pushed them down the steps. What we did not realize was that they made a lot of noise that lasted for a long time. Grandmother, thinking the worst, started praying to Saint Spyridon - the guardian Saint of Corfu - from her bedroom, asking for help. And my irate grandfather came storming out of his room, demanding to know what was happening. We said that some potatoes had gotten away from us. We apologized and promised to be careful next time.

Dalia and I picked up the potatoes and put them back into the bucket. But when we returned to the top of the stairs, Dalia turned to me and asked, with a twinkle in her eye, "Same game?" I nodded my head yes and let the potatoes roll down the steps again.

Grandfather reported us to Mother. Dalia was sent home and she was not allowed to come to our house for one week. I was grounded for the same amount of time.

However, this did not change our relationship. We have remained friends throughout the years.

POTATOES WITH TOMATO SAUCE (POTATOES YAHNI)

Makes 4 servings

2 pounds potatoes (2 large potatoes)
1 medium onion sliced
2 - 4 tablespoons oil
6 tablespoons tomato sauce
Salt and pepper to taste
1 cup water

In a skillet, sauté onions in oil. Peel, slice or cube the potatoes. Add water and tomato sauce to the onions. Add potatoes. Cook over medium heat until potatoes are cooked and the liquid is absorbed. I like to stir the mixture while it is cooking in order to avoid sticking. Additional water can be added to avoid sticking.

Potatoes Yahni can be eaten as a meal along with a side dish of feta cheese.

Yahni is a Turkish term that refers to a dish cooked on low heat. Many vegetables can be cooked this way, such as okra or green beans.

EASY GREEN BEANS AND TOMATOES

Makes 8-10 servings

2 cans of green beans (2 pounds or less)

2 cans sliced tomatoes

3/4 cup oil

1 onion chopped

Pepper and garlic salt to taste

Sauté the onion in part of the oil. In a saucepan, place tomatoes and drained green beans. Add the sautéed onions and the rest of the oil. Cook over a low heat until all ingredients are mixed and liquid is reduced.

VARIATION: Add corn and you have a succotash dish. Also, sliced carrots can be added.

MIXED VEGETABLE CASSEROLE (BRIAM)

Makes 10-12 servings

2 - 3 medium potatoes

2 - 3 medium zucchini squash

1 large eggplant

2 - 3 green peppers

3 - 4 tomatoes

2 - 3 onions

Salt and pepper to taste
1/2 cup parsley finely chopped
1/2 cup to 3/4 cup oil
2 teaspoons tomato paste diluted in some water

Parsley can be substituted with 2 teaspoons chopped spearmint.

Wash vegetables and remove stem ends. Cut vegetables into chunks and mix them in a bowl. Place them in an oiled baking pan. Add the oil, parsley, tomato paste and water. Add the salt and pepper. Bake in a moderate oven for one hour or until the liquid is absorbed.

VARIATION: Cut vegetables into medium-size slices. Slice zucchini lengthwise. Layer the potatoes, eggplant, peppers and zucchini. Between layers, add onions, cut tomatoes, chopped parsley, tomato paste, water, salt and pepper. Bake in a moderate oven until liquid is absorbed.

VARIATION: Instead of using all of the first four ingredients, use potatoes and eggplant or potatoes and zucchini plus all the other ingredients can be used.

Briam can be served as a main dish with feta cheese on the side.

Briam is a Turkish style dish which was probably introduced by Greeks who fled to Corfu from the Turkish-occupied mainland.

VEGETABLES

STUFFED TOMATOES

Makes 6 servings

12 medium tomatoes
1 pound hamburger
1/2 cup rice (uncooked)
4-6 tablespoons oil or more
1/2 cup chopped parsley or dill or a combination
2 small onions chopped fine
1 egg
Pulp from tomatoes
Salt and pepper to taste
Water (will vary based on tomatoes' juiciness and the size of the pan)

Optional
1/2 cup raisins
1/2 cup pine nuts

Cut off tops of tomatoes. Put them aside to later use as lids. Scoop out the pulp of the tomatoes and pour into saucepan. Add some water and bring to a boil. Set it aside. If tomatoes are too acidic, add 1/2 teaspoon of sugar. Add the other ingredients. Pour tomato pulp through a sieve and add to the mixture. Fill each tomato with the mixture and cover with a tomato lid. Place in a casserole dish and add water. Bake for 30-40 minutes until the rice is cooked, while basting occasionally. Add more water if needed. Tomatoes will produce their own juice.

I remember that Mother would sometimes substitute peppers for tomatoes and use this filling. But her preference was tomatoes.

STEWED LEEKS

Makes 4-5 servings

2 pounds leeks
1 large onion sliced
2 tablespoons tomato paste diluted in water
1/2 cup oil
Salt and pepper to taste

Clean leeks. Cut off roots and coarse tops. Discard outer leaves. Cut them into pieces, 2 inches long and wash thoroughly. Place cut leeks and onions in a pan. Cover them with water in which you have diluted the tomato paste. Add the oil and seasoning. Cover the pan and cook over low heat until the leeks remain with their own sauce.

VEGETABLES COOKED IN OIL (LATHERA)

A very common method of cooking vegetables is cooking with tomato sauce, onion and a lot of oil. Greeks like oil in their dishes and use it with abundance. Because we generally don't use butter on our bread, we dip our bread in oil. Oil is an integral part of the Mediterranean diet. When I return home during the summers, I find that I am no longer accustomed to using such large quantities of oil in my food. So, I pour out much of it. This is the reason that I am giving you a range of oil quantities in

the recipes. Start with the lesser amount of oil and then add more if you prefer.

Oil with a tomato sauce or tomato paste will make the sauce thicker and more substantial.

Vegetables cooked in oil are called "lathera" which means oily in Greek. There are many vegetables that can be made into lathera. The most popular ones are green beans, okra, leeks and potatoes. Cabbage, eggplant, cauliflower, green peas and zucchini can be cooked in the same manner.

ARTICHOKES IN OIL

Makes 4-6 servings

Back home, we cooked the same dish with fresh artichokes from our garden, which was very time-consuming.

4 - 6 tablespoons oil

1/2 onion sliced

1 cup frozen green peas

2 medium potatoes sliced

1 can artichoke hearts (10-12 ounces)

Juice of 1 lemon

Water

Salt and pepper to taste

2 tablespoons fresh dill

Sauté the onions in oil, stirring occasionally. Add the peas, potatoes, lemon juice, seasoning and enough water to cover. Bring mixture to a boil and then add artichokes and dill. Cook slowly for 30-40 minutes.

Spoon Preserves

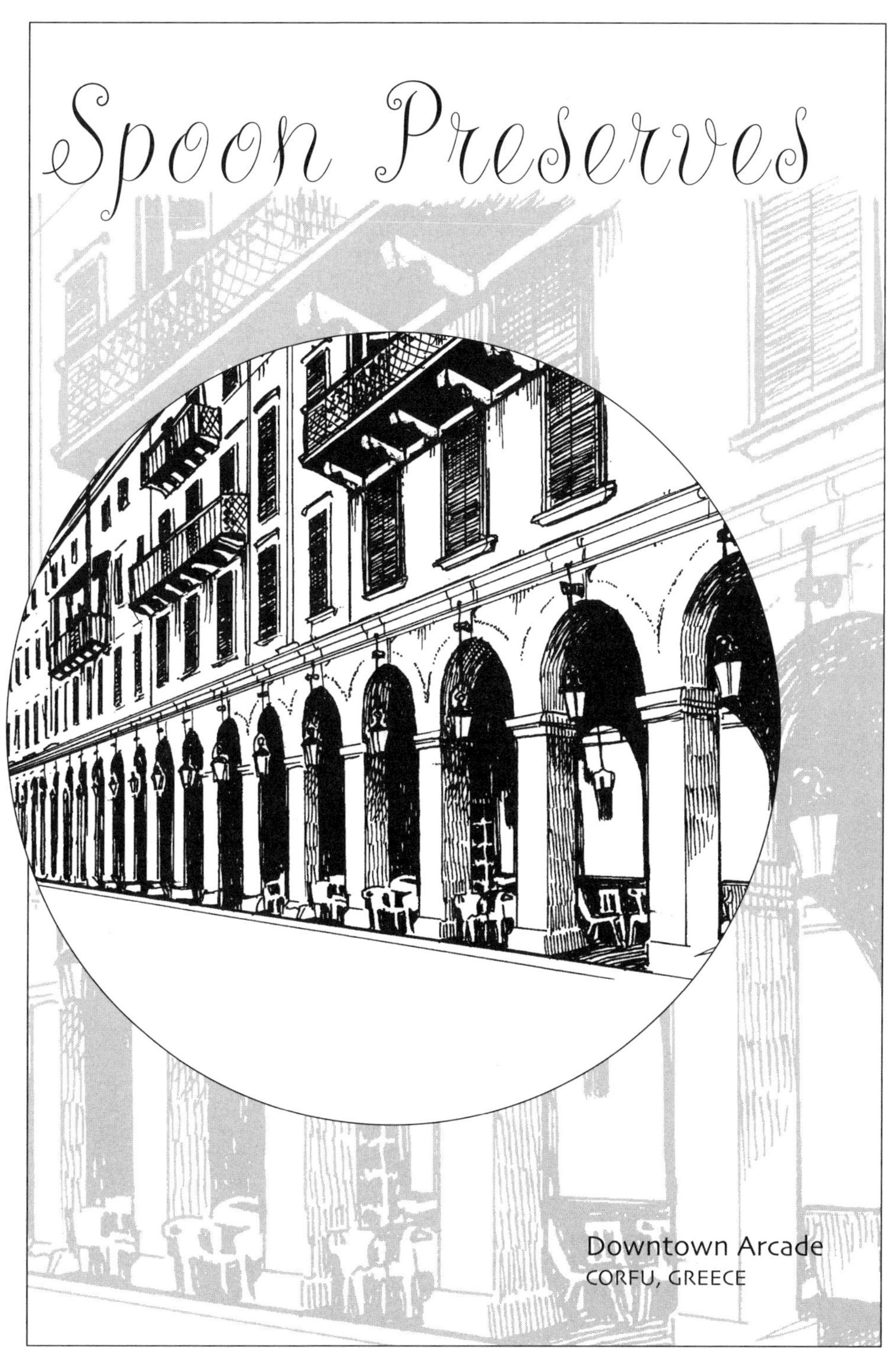

Downtown Arcade
CORFU, GREECE

PRESERVES

Greece produces many - and wonderful - fruits, some not known to Americans. Our garden had many varieties of fruit. Mother had some experience in grafting and pruning. Our trees flourished under her care. Except for syrups and preserves, we dried our fruit under the sun. Apricots, pears, figs and plums were our favorites. My mother would cut the fruit in thin slices, arrange them on a board and cover them with a cheesecloth. It was my assignment to turn them over and chase away the bees.

Another favorite preserve of ours was tomato paste. We started with tomato juice placed in a large platter. The sun dried the juice into a paste that we preserved with salt and a layer of oil on top.

SPOON PRESERVES

It is a Greek tradition that whenever guests visit a Greek home they will be served a glass of water and a spoonful of preserves served in a fancy glass or crystal saucer. The guest eats the preserves with a spoon and drinks the water, then returns the spoon to the empty glass. Every possible fruit can be used for the preserves. Sweet and sour cherries, quince, pears, apricots, strawberries and grapes are possibilities. The peel of sweet or bitter oranges, special lemons, and watermelons can also be used. Not well-known in the United States are baby eggplant, cherry tomato and green bitter orange preserves. Even nuts at the very early stages of ripening can be used. The process for making these preserves is labor-intensive but the results are worth it.

I am including the recipes for grape and quince preserves because both were grown in my garden.

GRAPE PRESERVES

For every cup of grapes use 1/2 cup sugar
Juice of 1 lemon

Use whole seedless grapes or remove the seeds.

Put grapes in a saucepan with enough water to cover them. Simmer until grapes are soft but not mushy. Add the sugar and lemon juice and continue to simmer until the liquid is absorbed and the syrup is set. Let it cool. Store in glass jars and seal.

SPOON PRESERVES

QUINCE PRESERVES

Makes 4 cups

4-6 quinces
1 cup of sugar for every cup of cooked quince
Juice of 1 lemon
Water

Wash and peel the quince. Discard the cores. Cut the fruit into thin slices or grate. Put in a saucepan and cover with water. Simmer until tender, 1 - 1 1/2 hours. Then add the sugar and lemon juice and cook on a low heat until the syrup thickens. Stir occasionally. Test the syrup by placing a few drops onto a saucer. If the drops do not spread, the syrup is set. Cool the preserves and store in glass jars.

If you want to make a quince syrup, grate the fruit and simmer in water until tender. Pass it through a food mill or cheesecloth. Measure the liquid and add one cup of sugar for every cup of liquid. Add the lemon and simmer until the syrup thickens.

Desserts & Breads

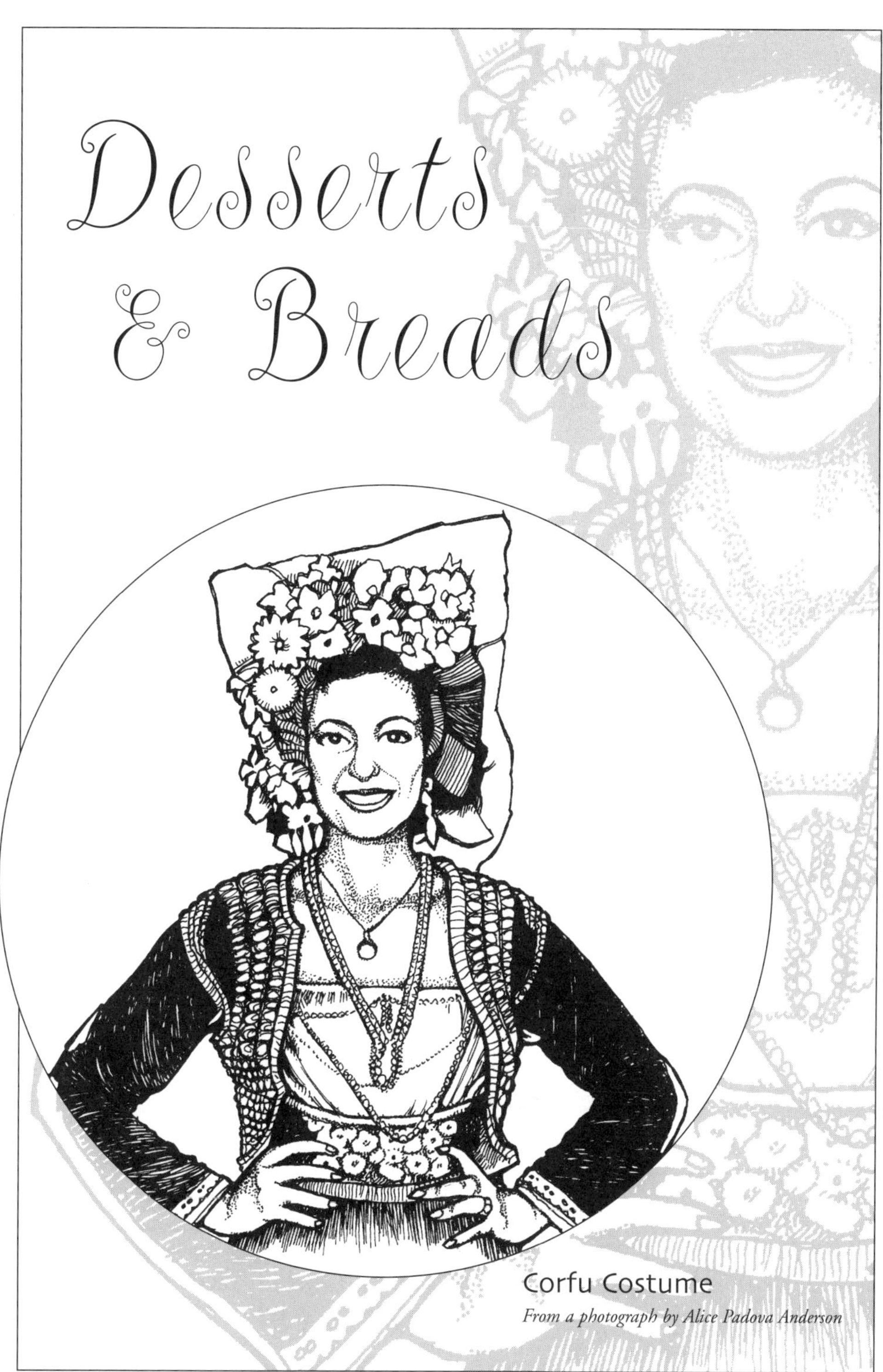

Corfu Costume

From a photograph by Alice Padova Anderson

DESSERTS & BREADS

ABOUT CAKES

I have always mixed my cakes by hand. I developed this habit because there was not a mixer in my house during the 1940's and 1950's. And, I beat the egg whites with a hand egg beater which required a lot of time. When I eventually tried to introduce some modern appliances into my mother's kitchen, she would seldom use them. You will discover that my cakes have a coarse texture. If you use a mixer, they will become smoother, but they will lose a certain textural quality. I now use a mixer to beat the egg whites and to blend some of the ingredients in a cake, but I don't do it very often.

Mother's cake recipes came from friends, and from the cookbooks available at the time. In fact, many of Mother's cakes were named after her friends. Through her cakes, certain aspects of my mother's life unfolded before me. I learned about her circle of friends and relatives, on what occasions she visited them and whose recipes she felt were worthy of including in her red notebooks.

I noticed that none of the cakes had a frosting. I don't know if it was the custom not to frost or if sugar was too expensive. Powdered sugar is sometimes used on a few of the cakes. Be careful and don't use soda instead of sugar, which my aunt mistakenly did one time. You can imagine the disastrous results.

Many of the cakes' ingredients and meal recipes came from my family's garden. Oranges and lemons were used in quantities unfamiliar to the American taste. It was very common for Mother to use the peel of one or two lemons at a time. If she was short a lemon, Mother would send me out into the garden to cut more lemons. But she used spices sparingly because they were expensive or not readily available. I have tried to preserve Mother's traditional recipes and also translate them into American measurements for your convenience.

Mother maintained her cooking style over the years. In the 1950's she finally discontinued using her homemade oven. The oven was a contraption made of tin that would open in the middle. It had a rack at the bottom that would hold one pan at a time. The oven was placed directly over the coals. Mother's original recipes described in detail how she worked with this oven. Although it required time to warm up, the final results were usually tasty and well-done.

TIPS FOR PREPARING CAKES

When using a tube cake pan, use one with a solid bottom. When baking a cake, test whether or not it is done by inserting a sharp knife or a toothpick. If it comes out clean, the cake is done. When using raisins, sprinkle them with flour so that they don't sink to the bottom of the pan.

Although Greeks love pastries they are not necessarily a part of the everyday Greek meal. Greeks will frequently end a meal with fruit and the traditional Greek coffee.

The rich pastries that are associated with Greek cuisine are reserved for guests and special occasions such as feasts and holidays. A good hostess will never allow visitors to leave her house without serving them a pastry, a preserve, Greek coffee, a liqueur and a glass of water.

Greek pastry shops serve the traditional sweets, some of which are made with phyllo and syrup such as baklava, galatoboureko and revani. The fancy shops offer a variety of pastries that we call Pastas. They are a variety of tort pastries that contain a lot of sugar, butter and cream.

On several recipes, I have reduced the amount of sugar which makes the cake less sweet than some Americans are used to.

Note: Most of my cake recipes yield 16-20 pieces.

DESSERTS & BREADS

ALMOND BALLS

Makes 5 dozen

1 pound ground blanched almonds
3 cups finely crushed toast (see note)
2 cups sugar
1/4 cup cocoa
1 1/2 cups water
1/4 cup cognac
Granulated or powdered sugar

In a bowl, mix the almonds, toast, cocoa and one cup of sugar. Combine one cup of sugar and one and one-half cups of water in a pan. Cook for a few minutes. Remove from heat. Add the cognac and the other ingredients. Mix thoroughly with a wooden spoon. Shape mixture into 1-inch balls and roll in granulated or powdered sugar. Arrange in a container and refrigerate for one day before serving.

If the dough is too stiff, add more water or cognac. If the dough is too soft, add toast.

If desired, other alcoholic beverages such as rum, bourbon, or ouzo can be used.

For a delicate taste, substitute lemon juice for cognac and add grated lemon peel.

Note: Toast in packages may be found in health food stores or other specialty shops.

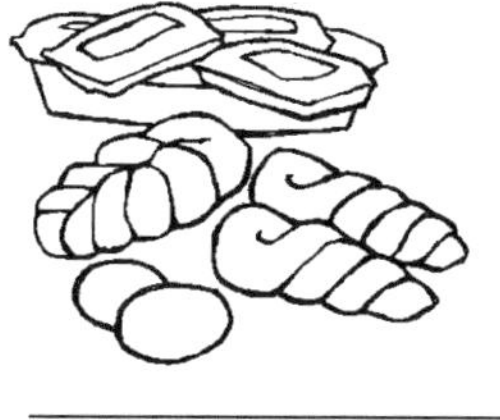

ANISE CAKE

2 sticks butter
2 cups sugar
4 cups flour
4 eggs
1 cup milk
1 cup golden raisins
2 tablespoons cognac
3 teaspoons baking powder
Grated peel of 1 lemon
Grated peel of 1 orange
4 tablespoons anise seed

Cream the butter and sugar together. Add the eggs and beat the mixture until well-blended. Add the cognac, lemon peel, orange peel and anise.

Sift the flour with the baking powder and add it gradually to the batter while alternating pouring in the milk. Sprinkle the raisins with flour and add to the mixture. Beat the batter a few minutes so that all ingredients are blended. Pour into a greased and lightly floured tube or bundt pan. Bake at 350° for one hour.

ABOUT PHYLLO

If the phyllo is frozen (generally this is how it is found in the grocery store) put it in the refrigerator and let it thaw over a 12-hour period. Then, take out of the refrigerator and allow to sit at room temperature for two more hours before using.

When you work with phyllo sheets, cover them with a plastic wrap and a dampened towel. Keep them covered except when you are removing the sheets, one at a time.

Most commercial phyllo comes in one-pound packages. A package will contain 20-25 rectangular sheets measuring 11" x 15."

For desserts such as baklava, lightly butter one sheet at a time with a pastry brush and place in a well-buttered baking pan. Repeat the procedure with as many phyllo sheets as the recipe requires. Put filling in the middle of the phyllo sheets or in layers between pastry sheets. And, top it with the remaining pastry sheets.

For triangles (cheese, spinach, etc.) layer as many phyllo sheets as you are going to use. Cut into strips five inches wide. Butter each strip.

Put a teaspoon of the filling one inch from the end nearest to you. Fold the phyllo in order to form the triangles. Seal the last triangle with a little water. If baking, place the sealed side down on an ungreased cookie sheet and bake.

HOMEMADE PHYLLO

Makes five sheets of phyllo

3 cups flour

1 tablespoon olive oil

2/3 cup lukewarm water

1 teaspoon salt

Two tablespoons of butter can substitute for the oil. Butter will make the dough softer.

Sift the flour and salt together. Add the oil and water to make a firm dough. Knead dough until smooth and elastic. Let it rest for one hour. Take pieces of the dough and roll them on a floured board until paper thin. Leave them for three quarters of an hour to dry. Cover phyllo sheets with waxed paper and use in the recipes of your choice. Phyllo sheets will need to be cut to accommodate various pan sizes.

DESSERTS & BREADS

BAKLAVA

Makes 35-40 pieces

1 pound phyllo pastry (one package)
3 4-ounce packages walnuts
3 4-ounce packages almonds (all walnuts or all almonds can be used)
1 4-ounce box Zwieback
1/2 cup sugar
1 1/2 teaspoons cinnamon
1 teaspoon cloves
1 pound sweet butter (unsalted)
Whole cloves for decoration

Syrup

3 cups sugar
3 cups water
1 cup honey
Juice of one lemon

Cut almonds and walnuts into small pieces. Put Zwieback between two pieces of waxed paper and crush with a rolling pin. Place the above ingredients in a bowl. Add sugar, cinnamon and cloves. Mix well and let stand for a few hours.

Line an 11 x 17 rectangular, buttered, baking pan with a sheet of phyllo. Brush with melted butter. Add 3-4 more phyllo sheets the same way. Sprinkle 4 or more tablespoons of the mixture on the phyllo. Cover with 2 buttered sheets.

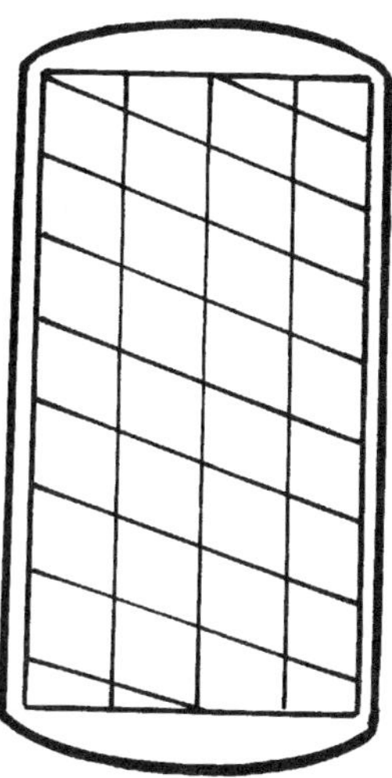

Repeat the same procedure until all ingredients are used (4-5 layers). Cut baklava into diamond shape pieces with a sharp knife (see illustration). Insert a whole clove in the middle of each diamond for decoration and flavor.

Bake at 300° for one hour or until golden brown.

For the Syrup

Pour the sugar and water into a saucepan. Let it simmer for 10-15 minutes. Add the lemon juice and the honey and let it simmer for 5 more minutes. Honey is added last to avoid foaming. Remove from heat and cool.

Add cold syrup on hot baklava for better absorption. Allow to stand several hours before serving.

NOTES: This is a large recipe. Because it takes time to prepare baklava, I prefer making a large batch and sharing it with my friends.

I make my own crumbs. My method is to leave several pieces of white bread in the open for 1-2 days. I then cut them into pieces, pour them in a blender and mix to a crumb consistency.

Use the same method for other recipes that call for crumbs. Zwieback generally is sweeter than crumbs.

BUTTER COOKIES (KOULOURAKIA)

Makes 4-5 dozen depending on size

2 sticks butter softened
6 eggs
2 cups sugar
1 cup milk
3 teaspoons baking soda
Lemon peel grated
1 tablespoon cognac
12 cups of flour

For topping
1 egg beaten with 1 tablespoon water
Sesame seeds (optional)

Generally, koulourakia are crisp and not too sweet. Ouzo or vanilla can be substituted for cognac. Orange rind can be substituted for lemon rind. The combinations depend on the preferences and imagination of the cook.

Cream butter and gradually add the sugar. Beat eggs lightly and add to the butter mixture. Mix thoroughly. Add cognac, grated rind of lemon and mix well. Sift together flour and baking soda. Alternately add the milk and flour. Beat well after each addition. Beat the last few cups of flour by hand until you get a soft dough. Break off small pieces of the dough and roll on a floured board to form a dough rope 1/3 to 1/2

inch thick, depending on how thick you want the koulourakia. Be consistent in the thickness so that all the cookies will bake at the same time.

Form dough into desired shapes. Brush with beaten egg and water to give a gloss or sprinkle the top with sesame seeds. You can also spread sesame seeds on a plate and press one side of each cookie into the seed mixture.

Arrange on an ungreased cookie sheet. Bake for 20 minutes at 350° or until golden brown.

Koulourakia can be stored in tin containers. They will keep fresh for 2 - 3 months.

DESSERTS & BREADS

KOULOURAKIA (CRISP)

Makes 3 dozen

1 cup butter (2 sticks)
6 eggs
1 1/2 cups sugar
8 cups flour
1 teaspoon baking soda or less
1 - 2 tablespoons vanilla
Confectioners sugar

Beat the butter, gradually adding the sugar and vanilla. Beat the eggs slightly, adding in the baking soda. Add to the butter mixture. Blend well. Add the flour and make a smooth dough. Form dough into desired shapes and put on ungreased baking sheet. Bake in the oven at 350° for about 20 minutes or until done. Dip koulourakia into confectioners sugar while they are hot.

MOTHER'S KOULOURAKIA

Makes 4-5 dozen

2 1/2 sticks unsalted butter
6 eggs
2 cups sugar
1 cup milk
3 teaspoons baking soda
12 cups flour
2 tablespoons vanilla or peel of one lemon or one orange

For topping
1 egg beaten with 1 tablespoon water

Cream the butter. Add the sugar. Beat eggs lightly and add them to the mixture. Add vanilla or peel of your choice. Blend well. Add the milk with the baking soda, alternating with the flour, and make a soft dough. Shape dough with lightly floured hands into desired shapes and arrange on ungreased cookie sheet. (See diagram for shapes. Also use your own imagination.) Be consistent with the thickness of the koulourakia so that they can bake evenly. Brush with beaten egg and water mixture to give them a shine. Bake in a moderate oven at 350° for 20 minutes or until golden brown.

Koulourakia can be stored in a tight tin can. They will stay fresh for 2 - 3 months.

The Cake Story

While in the United States, I finished a master's in home economics with a minor in nutrition. One of the courses I was required to take was Experimental Foods. It was my luck to have to prepare a cake. The cake called for two level teaspoons of baking powder. As I was not familiar with the measurements, I used two rounded tablespoons of baking powder. I put my cake in the oven and checked it regularly through the glass door. Very soon I saw my cake swelling like a tide and waves of dough started to overflow the pan, landing at the bottom of the oven and starting to burn. Concerned, I called the instructor and told her that something was wrong with the cake. "Impossible!" she exclaimed. "This is a standard cake!"

With a grin on my face I told her, "Unfortunately, you don't have a standard student!" Needless to say, the "standard" cake was discarded. Nothing was left to eat or to share. After this incident I learned the meaning of STANDARD and I managed to finish the class with a grade of B.

CAKE ASPASIAS

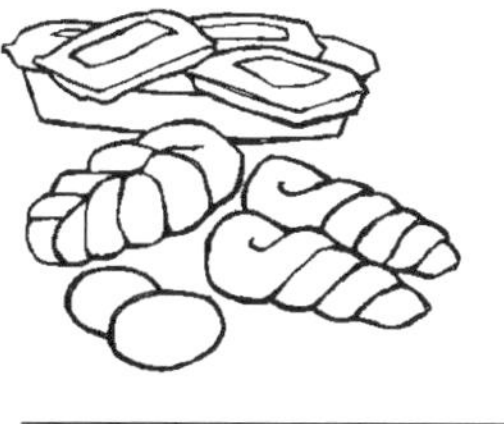

3 cups flour
1 1/2 cups sugar
3 eggs
1 stick butter
1 cup raisins (black or golden)
1 teaspoon baking powder
1 teaspoon baking soda
Peel and juice of 1 orange
1/2 cup milk

Cream the butter and sugar together. Add the eggs and beat until well-blended. Add the milk, the orange juice and the orange peel. Mix well. Sift the flour, baking powder and soda together and gradually add to the batter. Sprinkle the raisins with 1-2 tablespoons of flour so that they will not fall to the bottom of the cake. Add them to the mixture. If the dough seems too stiff, add a little milk. Pour into a well-greased and lightly-floured tube pan and bake at a moderate temperature for 45 minutes to 1 hour.

CAKE FROSOS

4 cups flour
2 cups sugar
3 eggs
1 cup (2 sticks) butter
1 cup milk
1 cup golden raisins
1/2 teaspoon baking powder
1/2 teaspoon baking soda
1 tablespoon cognac
Peel and juice of 1 orange

Cream butter and sugar until light and fluffy. Add the eggs and beat until well-blended. Add the cognac, orange juice and peel. Beat until batter is creamy and smooth. Sift the flour with the baking powder and soda and gradually add to the batter, alternating with the milk and raisins. Before adding the raisins, sprinkle them with 1-2 tablespoons of flour so that they will be evenly distributed in the batter.

After ingredients are well-mixed, pour into a greased and lightly floured tube pan or bundt pan. Bake at 350° for about 1 hour.

Lizeta's Story

Lizeta was short, plump, energetic and spirited with a twinkle in her eye. She was always wearing high heels with thin spikes that could hardly carry her weight.

The oldest child of three, Lizeta would organize the household, the family activities and family finances. She learned how to play the piano early in life which, in my culture, was a sign of good upbringing. My mother told me that Lizeta was a great pianist. When she was sitting at the piano, Lizeta's demeanor became gentle and sentimental, although she could be bold and aggressive.

"Lizeta traveled extensively, giving concerts all over Greece, making friends and attracting admirers."

My mother knew Lizeta and her family. Mother's aunt lived next door to Lizeta. During the weekly visits to her aunt, mother visited Lizeta and her family.

Lizeta's family was living in a three-story house with a big magnolia tree in the yard. The house was well-kept and decorated with the finest furniture. Watercolors and etchings painted by local artists were hanging from the walls. A grand piano filled the salon on the first floor where Lizeta practiced for hours. The kitchen and dining area were on the first floor. There was an aviary on the back patio. Lizeta and her family loved birds. Canaries would sing all day long as cats would watch them fly, protected in their enclosure.

A long, sweeping staircase with a colonnade banister reached to the second floor where the bedrooms were located. On the third floor an attic was reserved for the servants' quarters. Lizeta's family could afford two servants, a maid and a cook and occasional part-time help.

Lizeta traveled extensively, giving concerts all over Greece, making friends and attracting admirers.

A story was told that Lizeta could give the "evil eye." Cakes would fall flat in her presence, flowers would wilt under her gaze and people would trip and fall if she would look at them maliciously. My cousin remembers a very specific incident. Lizeta was visiting her and my cousin's servant entered the room with a pot of flowers. When Lizeta said to her, "What beautiful flowers," the servant froze and dropped the very expensive vase.

There were many stories about Lizeta. She is remembered as being bold, decisive and quick in action. Mother remembers a story that reflects Lizeta's spirit. When the Germans bombarded Corfu and dropped incendiary bombs that burned half of Corfu Town, Lizeta was on the alert. One night, a bomb fell on the roof of her household. Lizeta lost no time. Carrying a bucket of earth, she climbed out of a narrow passage to the roof and extinguished the bomb's fire.

With a gesture of disgust she kicked the bomb off the roof and thus saved the beautiful house which stands as a memorial to her bravery.

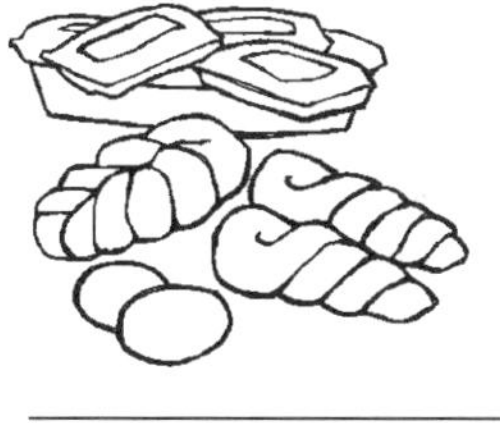

CAKE LIZETAS

2 sticks butter
3 cups flour
1 1/2 cups sugar
5 eggs
1 teaspoon baking powder
5 ounces fruitcake mix
3/4 to 1 cup golden raisins
1/2 teaspoon nutmeg
Grated peel of 1 lemon
1/4 pound almonds cut into small pieces

Cream butter and sugar together until light and fluffy. Add the eggs and beat by hand until well-blended. Sift the flour with the baking powder. Set aside. Sprinkle the raisins with some of the flour. Add the other ingredients. Then add the flour in small amounts, mixing well after each addition. If the batter is too thick add a little bit of milk. Pour into a buttered and floured tube or bundt cake pan. Bake at 350° for one hour.

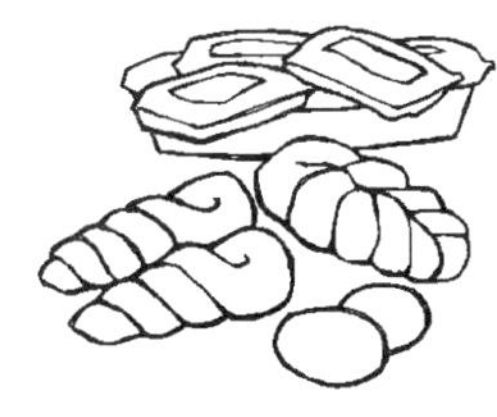

CAKE WITH ORANGES

1 1/2 sticks of butter
2 cups sugar
5 cups flour
6 eggs
1 teaspoon baking soda
Juice of 4-5 oranges (one cup liquid)
Grated peel of 1 orange
Grated peel of 1 lemon

Cream butter and sugar together. Add the eggs and beat until well-blended. Add lemon and orange peel. Dissolve the soda in the orange juice. Alternately add flour and orange juice. If the batter is too thin, add a little more flour. Pour into a well-greased and lightly-floured tube cake pan and bake in oven at 350° for 50 to 60 minutes.

CAKE WITH YOGURT

2 cups sugar
1 cup butter (2 sticks)
6 eggs
1 cup yogurt drained
3 - 3 1/2 cups of flour
Grated rind of 1 lemon
2 tablespoons cognac
1 1/4 teaspoon baking soda

Cream butter and sugar until light and fluffy. Add the eggs and beat until well-blended. Add the cognac, lemon peel and yogurt. Use mixer for better blending of the yogurt with the other ingredients. Sift the flour with the baking soda and add small quantities into the mixture while blending and stirring. Pour into a greased and lightly floured bundt or tube pan. Bake at 350° for 45 minutes.

Use plain yogurt that is thick and sour. If it has excess liquid, drain yogurt using a cheesecloth if necessary. Because the drained yogurt is thick, the cake may require less flour. If the yogurt is thin, you will need to use all the flour asked for in the recipe.

Victoria's Story

Victoria was a beautiful woman, tall, slender and straight like a cypress. Some people called her an Amazon or a Cariatide, which she accepted with grace.

She had a long face with thick eyebrows, a sensuous mouth and penetrating eyes. Her hair was braided and placed around her head in various and interesting patterns. The woman was always well-groomed and impeccable in her dress with special little touches that added distinction and class.

"From the house, one could see acres and acres of olive trees interspersed among tall, thin cypress trees that were reaching for the sky..."

Victoria married into money. Her husband, John, had a large estate in one of the villages near Corfu Town. They built a large, simple house on the property. Inside was a toilet and running water, which was considered quite modern at the time.

From the house, one could see acres and acres of olive trees interspersed among tall, thin cypress trees that were reaching for the sky; a typical Corfu landscape. Grapevines had been planted on the hillsides and orange and kumquat trees surrounded the house.

Because the estate was large, farm hands frequently worked on the property, particularly during the olive-picking season. Two families lived permanently on the acreage. They provided a variety of skilled and unskilled services for both the house and the farm. John had an olive press built on the estate and used it to process olives for himself and his neighbors.

First, the olives were placed in a round enclosure and crushed by three large, heavy millstones operated by a mechanism tied to a horse who would walk in circles. The crushed olives were then packaged in heavy burlap bags and stacked one on top of the other. Finally, the bags were pressed, which produced the golden oil of Corfu.

The relatives on my grandmother's side of the family had many things in common with Victoria's family. Grandmother's brother was a landowner with acres of olive trees and a vineyard. As well, he owned an oil press and a wine cellar. Many of the relatives made their own wine. As a matter of fact, I recall a family story about these two friends being found, inebriated, on the cellar floor.

At harvest time, Mother and her extended family would board a horse carriage, drive to Victoria's estate and stay for days. Stomping on the grapes contained in a big tub was one of the many enjoyable and unforgettable activities during their stay.

My relatives kept in touch with Victoria's family for many years and exchanged visits during holidays and other special occasions.

Corfu Landscape

From a photograph by Alice Padova Anderson

CAKE VICTORIAS (COCONUT CAKE)

1 stick butter

1 1/4 cup coconut shredded

5 eggs

2 cups flour

1 cup sugar

3/4 cup evaporated milk

3 teaspoons baking powder

1/2 teaspoon salt

2 - 3 tablespoons vanilla

Syrup (Optional)

2 cups sugar

2 cups water

Juice of half large lemon

Grated rind of 1 lemon

Cream butter and sugar until light and fluffy. In a separate dish, beat the eggs slightly and add them to the mixture. Add the coconut and evaporated milk and mix well.

Sift the flour, baking powder and salt together and gradually add to the batter. Add the vanilla last.

Pour batter into a 9-inch tube pan that has been buttered and sprinkled with flour. Using a fluted tube or bundt pan will give a more interesting appearance to the cake.

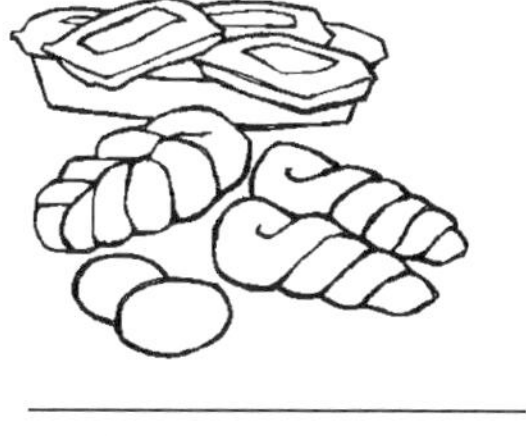

Bake at 350° for about one hour. Test with a knife.

Meanwhile, prepare the syrup. It should be cooled to room temperature. (See page 193.)

When cake is done, pour the cold syrup over hot cake. Let it cool and absorb the syrup. Then, turn it over onto a serving dish. A non-stick cake pan will give better results and provide easier handling.

I have prepared this cake with or without the syrup. I like it either way.

If you don't have a tube pan and you want to use syrup, you can use a 9 x 12 cake pan and cut the cake into squares.

LENTEN CAKE

6 cups flour
1 1/2 cups sugar
1 teaspoon cinnamon
1/2 teaspoon cloves
1/2 teaspoon nutmeg
1 tablespoon anise seed
1/4 pound almonds cut into small pieces
1/2 cup dark raisins
1/2 cup golden raisins
1 cup oil
Juice of 1 lemon
2-2 1/2 cups of water
2 tablespoons cognac
1 1/2 teaspoons baking soda
3 teaspoons baking powder
Sesame seeds to sprinkle on top

Sift flour into a bowl with all the spices, baking powder and soda. Sprinkle the raisins with a little of the flour mix. Add the oil to the flour and blend well. Make a well in the center of the dough. Add sugar and water in small amounts. Mix well after each additional ingredient. Add raisins, anise, almonds, lemon juice and cognac. If the dough is too stiff add a little water.

This is an oil cake with no eggs

Pour into a greased and floured tube pan. Sprinkle top with sesame seeds. Bake at 350° F for one hour.

NUT CAKE (KARYTHOPITA)

4 eggs
2 sticks butter
1 cup sugar
3 cups flour
1 tablespoon cinnamon
1 cup milk
2 cups ground English walnuts
3 teaspoons baking powder

Syrup

1 cup sugar
1 1/2 cups water
Juice of half lemon

Beat the sugar and butter together until light and fluffy. Add the eggs and beat until well-blended. Sift flour, baking powder, cinnamon and slowly fold into mixture, alternating with the milk. Gradually add the ground nuts. Blend well.

Pour mixture into a well-greased and lightly-floured 9 x 13 pan. Bake at 350° for 30-45 minutes. Watch carefully to avoid scorching. While still hot, top the cake with cold syrup.

MOTHER'S NEW YEAR'S CAKE

4 cups flour
2 sticks butter
1 1/2 cups sugar
4 eggs
1 cup milk
1 teaspoon baking powder
1 teaspoon baking soda
4 tablespoons cognac
Grated peel of 1 lemon
1 teaspoon salt
Sesame seeds for topping (optional)

Cream butter and sugar until light and fluffy. Add the eggs and beat to blend. Add the sugar, cognac and lemon peel. Sift the flour with the baking powder, baking soda and salt. Then, gradually add to the batter while alternating with the milk. After ingredients are well-mixed, pour into a greased and lightly-floured round baking pan. Sprinkle sesame seeds over the top of the batter.

Bake at 250° for one hour or until golden brown.

For good fortune, I add a coin. Whoever finds it will have good luck throughout the year. It is not so easy to find the coin because when the cake is cut for the New Year's meal, one piece is set aside for Christ, one piece for St. Basil (our Greek Santa), and one for the head of household. Sometimes a piece is cut and set aside for a poor person or a stranger who might walk in. This

I find that this order of cutting the cake varies from region to region. Here I describe what happened in my household.

demonstrates the spirit of hospitality in the Greek family. When the designated pieces are cut, the other members of the family are served. My family also decorated the table with twelve fruits and nuts. Some items we used for decorations included oranges, mandarin oranges, pomegranates, English walnuts, almonds, chestnuts, filberts, hazelnuts, peanuts, pistachios, dates, and figs.

MARBLE CAKE

2 cups sugar

2 sticks butter

4 cups flour

1 cup milk

7 eggs

2 tablespoons cognac

3 teaspoons baking powder

4 squares of Baker's semi-sweet chocolate (4 ounces) or 4 ounces of chocolate chips melted

Beat butter and sugar until light. Add eggs and cognac. Beat until very light and fluffy. Combine flour with baking powder and add to the mixture, alternating with milk. Melt chocolate in a double boiler. Add to half of the batter and pour the batter into a separate bowl. Spoon plain and chocolate batters alternately into a greased and lightly-floured bundt or tube pan.

Bake at 350° for one hour or until done.

EASTER BREAD

6 eggs
2 packages dry yeast
2 sticks unsalted butter
1/2 cup milk
1/4 cup water
2 tablespoons infusion of anise
1 teaspoon salt
3/4 cup sugar
6 cups of flour
Grated peel of half orange

For topping
1 egg beaten with 1 tablespoon water

Dissolve the yeast in lukewarm water. Add warm milk and 1/2 cup of flour. Mix well. Leave in a warm place and let it double in size. Add all ingredients and 3 1/2 cups of flour. Let rise for one hour. Punch it down. Add the rest of the flour. Knead it for five minutes. Make a ball and place it in a well-greased bowl. Leave for one hour. Punch it down again and knead it for an additional five minutes until the dough is smooth. Add a little more flour if needed. Form two loaves and place them on a greased baking sheet. Allow the loaves to rise for two hours. Beat an egg and brush the mixture on the surface of the loaves. When baked, the egg creates a glazed surface.

The traditional Easter breads fall under the cate-

gory of Tsourekia. Tsourekia are yeast breads, braided, with red dyed eggs for decoration and a shiny glaze. Although there are regional differences in the flavorings and the methods of braiding, they are always sweet.

In Corfu, we make a type of Tsoureki that is called Fogatsa. My Easter bread recipe is similar to the Fogatsa recipe.

I asked a friend, a Corfu restaurant owner, the difference between a Fogatsa and a Tsoureki. She told me that a Fogatsa has less sugar and is flavored with Masticha or Mahlepi.

Masticha is the sap of a bush. It is used as the primary ingredient in chewing gum and it is also used as flavoring for breads, liqueurs and cookies.

Mahlepi is the dried kernel of a wild cherry. It must be finely ground before it is used in cakes and breads.

With a Fogatsa dough we make the traditional Columbine. Colomba is the Italian word for dove. With part of the dough we make a braid eight inches long or longer. Flatten one end of the braid and place a red egg there. The egg is secured by using two strips of dough in a criss-

cross formation. At the top, where the strips meet, we insert colored feathers. I don't use the outside feathers of a hen or duck. Instead, I use the inside feathers which are softer and shorter.

When you make the loaf, insert a hard-boiled egg into the middle of the loaf before baking. With larger loaves, insert two or three eggs in the periphery of them. Bake at 325° for twenty minutes or until done. Although this bread does not require much sugar, it is still slightly sweet. Because of that, my diabetic friends like it very much. Instead of eggs, you can also decorate the bread with halved blanched almonds.

One time, I made the Columbine in my Missouri home. In order to get the real feathers, I plucked them from my neighbor's hens.

Of all the feasts celebrated in Greece, Easter is the most important. It always involves a good amount of cooking. Traditionally, dozens of eggs are dyed red and polished with oil. Red is the only color we use for which we have a special dye. The egg is a traditional symbol of Easter. A Christian holiday, Easter celebrates resurrection and new life. The red egg represents the potential for new life. The dove symbolizes innocence and purity.

It is a custom to try to break each other's egg by tapping them together. Anyone who has at least

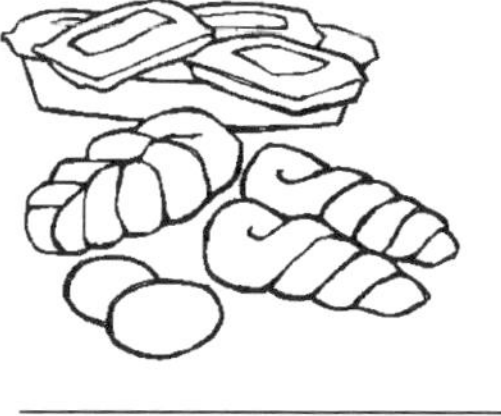

one solid end on his or her egg at the end of the party will be happy year round. Don't use a wooden egg.

FRITTERS OR HONEY PUFFS (LOUKOUMADES)

Makes 30 - 40

1 package dry yeast
4 cups flour
2 cups warm water
1 teaspoon sugar
1 teaspoon salt
Oil for frying
Sugar and cinnamon or honey for topping

Dissolve the yeast in 1/2 cup of warm water with the sugar. Add 1/2 cup more warm water and 1 cup of flour. Beat the ingredients to the consistency of a smooth cake batter. Leave the covered batter in a warm place for about an hour until it doubles in size. Add the remaining water, salt and enough flour to make a thick batter. Cover again and place the batter in a warm place. When it begins to bubble it is ready for frying. Heat oil in a deep frying pan. Once it becomes very hot, drop spoonfuls of the dough into the oil. Fry until puffed and golden brown. Remove loukoumades with a slotted spoon and place them on paper towels to drain. Serve hot with honey or dip them in sugar and cinnamon.

HOMEMADE PETA BREAD

Makes four 7-inch petas

2 cups whole wheat flour

1 package dry yeast

3/4 cup lukewarm water

1 teaspoon sugar

Dissolve yeast in the water. Add sugar. Combine the flour with the yeast. Mix and knead for seven minutes. Place in a bowl and cover. Let stand for 90 minutes. Punch it down and let the dough rise for another 45 minutes. Take a piece of the dough and roll it out at 1/8-inch thickness or more. Cut round pieces of rolled dough and place on a cookie sheet. Let them rise for another 30 minutes. Place the cookie sheet on the highest rack of the oven and let bake at 450° for 15 minutes. Peta will puff up but remain crisp. Don't expect them to be as soft as the commercial petas. Keep them in a plastic bag to conserve moisture and use them right away. Don't get discouraged if a couple don't puff, and don't compare them to the commercial petas.

KOURABIETHES

Makes 25 - 30

2 sticks unsalted sweet butter
1 cup confectioners sugar
1 egg yolk
1 tablespoon cognac
3 1/2 cups flour
1/2 teaspoon baking powder
Confectioners sugar for dusting

Whip butter until it is fluffy and white. Slowly add confectioners sugar, egg yolk and cognac. Mix well. Gradually add sifted flour and baking powder. Knead well until dough is smooth. Break small pieces of dough into the size of a walnut and shape them into circles or crescents. Inserting a clove in the middle of the cookie is optional. Place on a cookie sheet and bake at 350° for 15-20 minutes or until golden colored. While warm, roll kourabiethes in confectioners sugar. Sift confectioners sugar on top.

VARIATION: Add 1/2 cup blanched and finely chopped almonds to the dough.

Kourabiethes are favorite Greek cookies served at Christmas, New Year's and other festive occasions.

PLAIN HALVA

2 cups Cream of Wheat or farina

1 stick butter or 1/2 cup oil

Cinnamon to sprinkle over halva (optional)

1 cup pine nuts or 1 cup nuts or 1 cup raisins. Use them in the halva or on top of the halva

Syrup

2 cups sugar

4 cups water

2 sticks cinnamon (optional)

Heat the oil in a deep saucepan. Add the Cream of Wheat and stir continuously over low heat. When the mixture begins to brown, add the nuts or raisins. Stir until Cream of Wheat is a golden color. Cook syrup 5-10 minutes. Add the Cream of Wheat to the syrup and cook until thick. Cover the pan and let it stand 10 to 15 minutes. Pack the halva into a large mold or smaller individual molds. Turn into a serving dish. Garnish with cinnamon or nuts.

*Use the lowest possible heat and a long-handled wooden spoon because the mixture will bubble.

Halva looks very nice when poured into a fluted mold. I have also used jello molds in the past.

GALATOBOUREKO

Makes 12 pieces

6 cups of milk
2 cups Cream of Wheat
6 eggs
3/4 cup sugar
6 tablespoons butter
1/2 teaspoon salt
12 - 15 sheets of phyllo
Melted butter
Lemon peel to your taste

Syrup

2 cups sugar
2 cups water
1/4 cup honey
Lemon peel

I like to use pieces of lemon rind in the syrup which I discard after the syrup is done.

You can add 1/4 cup honey or substitute sugar for the honey to avoid making it too sweet. Add the honey at the last moment in order to avoid foaming.

Vanilla can be substituted for the lemon peel. But, I find that lemon peel gives it an exquisite and refined taste.

Heat milk with the butter, sugar and salt. Gradually add the Cream of Wheat, stirring con-

stantly. Bring the mixture to a boil and let it thicken to a custard consistency. Remove from heat. Beat eggs and fold into the farina mixture, stirring constantly. Add lemon peel. Cook the mixture for 3-5 minutes more. Set aside to cool while preparing the phyllo. Brush an 11 x 13 baking pan with melted butter. Line the pan with 5 - 6 individual buttered sheets of phyllo. Pour in the cooked custard. Cover with one sheet of phyllo. Brush with butter. Layer 5 more buttered sheets. Trim any uneven parts of phyllo with scissors. Cut through the top layer of phyllo into 12 or 16 pieces. Bake at 350° for 45 minutes to one hour. Test with a knife to see if done.

For the Syrup

Combine water and sugar. Add lemon peel. Boil for 10 minutes. Honey is to be added last. Cool syrup. Add cold syrup to hot pastry. You can also add hot syrup to cold pastry. When galatoboureko is done, cut through custard layer and bottom pastry. Follow the cuts you made before baking. Cool before serving.

ORANGE GALATOBOUREKO

Follow the basic recipe.

Instead of lemon peel use orange peel, 3 tablespoons of frozen orange juice diluted and 1 tablespoon vanilla.

GALATOBOUREKO DORAS

6 cups of milk
1 cup Cream of Wheat
1 cup sugar
6 eggs
12 - 15 sheets phyllo
6 tablespoons butter
1/2 teaspoon salt
Lemon peel or 1 tablespoon vanilla

Syrup
1 1/2 cups water
2 cups sugar
Lemon peel or 1 tablespoon vanilla

Follow the directions on the basic Galatoboureko recipe. Use vanilla instead of lemon peel or use both. This recipe makes a sweeter and lighter galatoboureko.

NOTE: I came across this recipe in my mother's notebook. On the side of the page Mother had a notation stating that the recipe was very good and had a delicious taste.

When writing down the recipe, I noticed that the milk was measured in "kartoucha" which is a Venetian measure of volume.

During a trip home to Corfu in the summer, I asked a number of people the meaning of kar-

I offer this recipe in memory of Dora, a good friend of my mother.

toucha. Although the younger people were unfamiliar with the term, an elderly woman knew the answer.

A kartoucho is one pint (2 cups).

I grew up with kartoucha. When the milk man passed through the neighborhood, his donkey loaded down with metal containers of milk, he would come to the door of our house and shout, "How many kartoucha do you need today?" Mother would come down to the door with a large pan and buy the milk for the day. She would boil the milk until it rose three times. This procedure was supposed to kill all of the bacteria. Because we had no refrigeration, the milk had to be consumed that day. With what was left, mother made a custard that she fed me in the afternoons.

Dora's Story

Dora and her sister, Anitsa, lived with their aunt Tzia Dorina in a house looking over the Garitsa Bay and the ancient castle near my mother's house. They all lived in my neighborhood of Anemomylos, the windmill. I don't remember ever meeting the sisters' parents who I think died before my birth, leaving Tzia Dorina to take care of the other females in the household. Tzia Dorina was a proper, elderly lady with her hair pulled back into a bun. She always wore dark clothing with white prints of polka dots or geometric designs. Dark clothing with a fine white print was considered respectable clothing for older women.

"...the jasmine bush remains standing and entices the neighbors with its delicate flowers and aroma."

I remember well their house which still stands. It is a two-story stucco structure with a jasmine bush in the backyard. When the jasmines were flowering, Mother would take me over for a visit with Tzia Dorina so that we could smell and admire the blossoms. We would always return with branches from the bush and put them into vases scattered around the house. Then when the flowers dried up we would collect them and put them in the linen drawers. They provided a fragrant smell for the sheets and pillowcases. Tzia Dorina, a very generous woman, gave us extra dried flowers which we put into small fabric bags and placed in the closets and drawers.

Although the sisters' house acquired various owners after the death of the sisters and Tzia Dorina, the jasmine bush remains standing and entices the neighbors with its delicate flowers and aroma. Anitsa never married, but Dora married a prominent doctor; a kind soul who looked after the poor to whom he gave free care. He delivered me at home and doctored me the first years of my life. I still remember him with his black bag and black hat that covered his white hair. He would frequently pass through the neighborhood, in a horse drawn carriage on his way to visit a patient. The doctor would wave but never stop. He was always too absorbed in thought. He died an old man but Dora remained alive for many more years.

Mother told many stories about Dora. Both went to a school for girls to become teachers. The school was located in the middle of Corfu Town, a half hour walk from home. A number of girls from the neighborhood attended the school. They would walk from house to house picking each other up along the way, and walk together to the school. Dora was always a problem because she was never ready. Some of the girls would wait for her while the others would walk ahead to school. They would tell tall tales to the headmistress about the reasons for the delay of the second group. The stories defied imagination. One time, they claimed that they saw some kittens drowning in the sea and tried to rescue them. Another time they told the teacher that they met an old man who apparently was lost and they took him home. The made-up stories were infinite and always full of good intentions.

PASTA FROLLA

In her original recipe notebook, my mother included this recipe for Pasta Frolla.

2 cups butter
1 cup sugar
4 cups flour
2 eggs
2 tablespoons cognac
Grated peel of 1 lemon
1/2 teaspoon baking powder
1 pound apricot jam

Cream butter and sugar together. Add eggs and beat until well-blended. Add cognac and lemon peel. Beat until combined. Stir in flour with baking powder. Form dough into a ball.

Line a 13 x 9-inch baking pan with foil to extend one inch beyond the ends of the pan. Grease foil. Put half of the dough into the bottom of the greased, foil-lined pan. Spread jam evenly over the dough. With the other half of the dough, form strips and place them diagonally over the jam. Form additional strips with the remaining dough and place them at right angles over the first layer of strips. Bake at 350° for about 30-40 minutes until golden brown. Cut into squares and remove foil.

The traditional filling for this dessert is apricot jam. I invite you to use the jam of your choice.

In many Greek cookbooks I discovered the recipe for Pasta Flora. In Corfu, we call it Pasta Frolla. The Italian word, frolla, means tender or soft.

An Italian friend of mine explained that the word refers to a soft dough that is not to be rolled.

ABOUT PANDESPANI

Pandespani is a light cake with lemon flavoring.

It was a Corfu custom to send a Pandespani covered on top with a lot of powdered sugar to the family of a newborn baby. I am not sure whether the custom exists today.

The word comes from an Italian phrase Pan di Spagna, bread of Spain, where it probably originated. I was told that when the Jews were expelled from Spain they took this cake recipe with them to the various countries where they settled.

My mother, who attended a French school run by French nuns, told me that when Marie Antoinette was asked what to feed the crowds she replied, in French, "Give them Pain d' Espagne" (give them cake).

Mother has always made Pandespani the traditional way. She would weigh eight eggs in their shells, add the same weight in sugar and half the weight in flour plus two tablespoons. Because she was very particular about those two tablespoons, mother would always remind me to add them. Making a Pandespani was a ritual for her and the entire family. Everything had to be done right.

When Mother came to the United States to visit me, I asked her several times to help me translate the recipe into American measurements using cups. She never made the translation because she insisted that her preparation method was the best. And, her cakes were always perfect. In the meantime, I was getting a headache. Pandespani became her trademark. My friends would ask for Mother's cake, the light yellow one with the lemon flavor. After many attempts and failures, I finally came up with a good recipe using American measurements which I incorporated in Pandespani II.

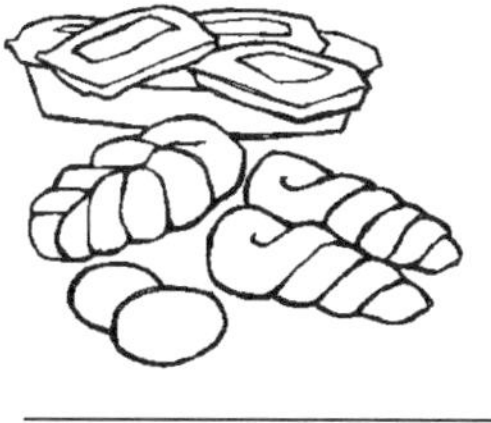

PANDESPANI I

8 eggs weighed with the shell
Equal weight of sugar
Half the weight of eggs in flour plus
 1 - 2 tablespoons
Grated rind of 1 lemon
Juice of 1 lemon

Beat the egg yolks with the sugar. Add lemon rind and lemon juice. Beat the egg white with an electric mixer at high speed until they form peaks. Alternately, add the egg whites and the flour, mixing from the bottom up rather than in a circular motion.

Bake in an angel food pan at 350° for 40 minutes or until done.

PANDESPANI II

8 eggs (extra large)

1 1/2 cups sugar

2 cups flour plus 2 tablespoons

Juice of 1 lemon

Grated peel of 1 lemon

Follow preparation directions for Pandespani I.

Mother would oftentimes use pandespani to make what she called a torte. She would make a thick custard and pour it over the cake. If Mother cut the cake into layers, she would pour some of the custard between them. Some people prefer the custard because it is not too sweet. I prefer spreading apricot jelly or preserves between the cake layers.

Custard

2 cups milk

1 egg

4 tablespoons sugar

2-3 tablespoons corn flour

Vanilla or other flavoring

Heat the milk. Add the egg beaten in sugar. Mix well. Add the corn flour and flavoring. Cook until thick.

PUDDING (PUDINGA)

Makes 12 servings

6 cups milk

2 cups Cream of Wheat

1 1/2 cups sugar

4 eggs

1 cup coarsely chopped nuts

3/4 cup raisins

3/4 cup golden raisins

1/2 stick butter

Lemon rind or orange rind grated

Pinch of salt

Heat milk with the butter, sugar and salt. Gradually add the Cream of Wheat while stirring constantly. Bring the mixture to a boil and let it thicken to a custard consistency. Beat eggs and fold into the Cream of Wheat mixture. Cook on a low heat for a few minutes. Remove from heat and cool. Add grated lemon or orange rind. Sprinkle raisins with a little flour and mix well so that they are coated. This prevents the raisins from sinking to the bottom of the batter. Stir raisins and nuts into the mixture. Pour into a 9 x 13 baking pan. Bake in a moderate oven at 350° for at one hour or more until done. Check with a knife.

Almonds can be substituted for other nuts. Make it sweeter by adding 1/4 cup sugar. Once cooked,

This recipe is a good example of the English influence in Corfu cooking.

a little rum, ouzo or cognac can be poured over.

The regular Cream of Wheat makes better custard.

This recipe comes from my mother's cousin. Every time we visited her, we were expecting a large piece of pudding. This dessert brings back memories of my Aunt Euterpe (the Greek muse of music), a favorite aunt of mine.

RICE PUDDING (RIZOGALO)

Makes 4 servings

4 cups milk
1 cup water
1/2 cup rice
1/2 to 3/4 cup sugar
Grated peel of 1 lemon
2 teaspoons cornstarch
1/2 teaspoon salt
Cinnamon to sprinkle on top

Boil rice in water for about 10 minutes. Add the milk and simmer for about 30 minutes, stirring frequently. Mix cornstarch with some water and pour it slowly into the pudding. Stir well for a few minutes. Add the sugar and salt and let it simmer for another 10-15 minutes. Remove from heat. Add the lemon peel, or vanilla if you like, and stir. Pour into individual dishes. Sprinkle with cinnamon. Eat it at room temperature or refrigerate prior to eating.

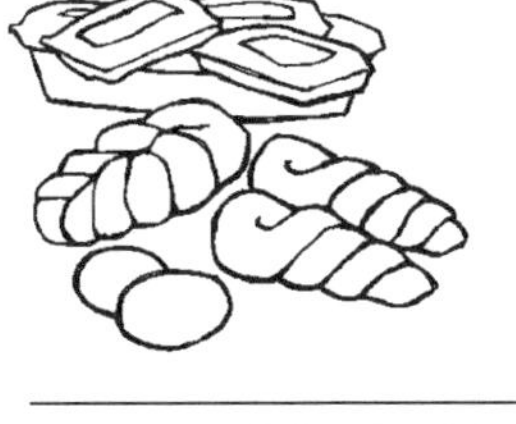

PUDDING WITH DRIED FIGS AND DATES

Makes 12-16 pieces

6 cups milk
2 cups Cream of Wheat
1 1/2 cups sugar
4 eggs
1 cup coarsely chopped nuts
8 - 10 dried figs cut into pieces
8 - 10 medium seedless dates cut into pieces
1/2 stick butter
Lemon rind grated
Pinch of salt

Follow directions for cooking the pudding on page 231.

Cut the figs into small pieces, 8 pieces a fig. Cut dates into pieces. Put them in a bowl. Sprinkle them with flour and mix so that they are well-coated. Add figs, dates and nuts into mixture. Pour into a 9 x 13 baking pan and bake in a moderate oven at 350° for at least an hour until done. Check with a knife.

This pudding will need a little more time to bake because the figs and dates add moisture.

SEMOLINA CAKE (REVANI)

Makes 12 - 16 pieces

2 cups flour
1 cup Cream of Wheat
6 eggs
1 cup sugar
3 sticks butter
3 - 3 1/2 teaspoons baking powder
1 cup orange juice
Grated rind of 1 orange

Syrup

3 cups sugar
2 cups water

Flavoring

Choose from brandy, vanilla or cinnamon

Cream butter and sugar together. Add the eggs and beat until well-blended. Add the Cream of Wheat, orange rind, orange juice and the flavoring of your choice. Sift the flour with the baking powder and add it gradually to the batter. Pour into a well greased and lightly floured 9 x 13-inch baking pan. Bake at 350° for 45 minutes to one hour.

For the syrup

Combine water and sugar. Boil 10 minutes and let it cool. Then, pour the syrup over hot cake and cut into squares.

TOT FAIT

Makes 12-16 pieces

15 graham crackers (two squares each)

2 cups sugar

2 tablespoons cognac

2 tablespoons cinnamon

8 eggs separated

Syrup

3 cups water

2 cups sugar

1 tablespoon cinnamon

2 tablespoons cognac

To crush the graham crackers, put them into a ziplock bag. Roll over them with a rolling pin into large crumbs. A mortar and pestle can be used. If you use a blender, make sure the crumbs are large.

In a bowl, beat the sugar with the egg yolks. Beat the egg whites until they form peaks and fold them into the egg-sugar mixture alternating with the graham cracker crumbs. Add cinnamon and cognac. Pour into a 9 x 13 ungreased pan. Bake at 350° for 45 minutes to 1 hour. Test with a knife.

For the syrup

Pour all the ingredients into a pan. Bring to a boil. Let it boil for 5-10 minutes. Remove from heat. Let it cool. Pour the cold syrup on top of the hot cake and let the cake absorb the syrup.

SEMOLINA COOKIES (MELOMAKARONA)

A TRADITIONAL CHRISTMAS COOKIE

Makes 50-60

2 cups oil
2/3 cups sugar
3/4 cup orange juice
2 tablespoons cognac
7-8 cups of flour
2 teaspoons baking powder
1 teaspoon baking soda
1 cup finely chopped nuts
For a spicy flavor, add nutmeg or cinnamon, cloves or a combination of the three.

Syrup

2 cups water
2 cups sugar
1 cup honey

Mix all ingredients together to make a stiff dough. Break off small pieces of the dough and shape into oblong forms about 2-2 1/2 inches long. Bake at 350° for 25-30 minutes until golden brown and then let cool. Bring syrup to a boil. Add the honey last because it foams. Dip the cold cookies in the warm syrup. Roll them in chopped nuts and spices.

VARIATION: You can place the hot cookies in a large pan and pour the cold syrup over them. Let them stand until the liquid is absorbed.

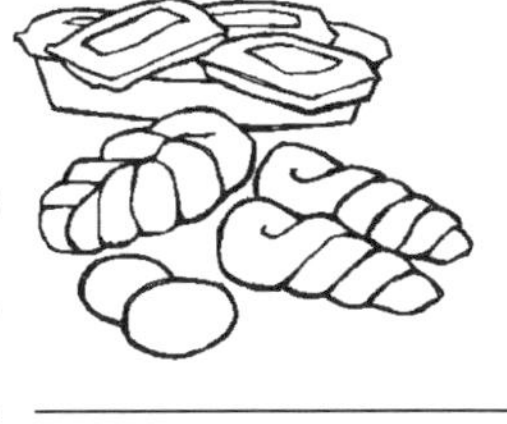

SWEET CORN BREAD (BARBAROPETA)

2 3/4 cups corn meal
2 cups boiling water
2 cups sugar
4 cups flour
2 sticks butter melted
2 tablespoons oil
2 eggs
Peel of 2 oranges
1/2 cup orange juice
1 cup golden raisins
1 cup raisins
1 cup nuts
1 1/2 teaspoon baking powder
2 tablespoons anise
4 tablespoons sesame seeds

Place the corn meal in a bowl. Pour the boiling water over it and mix well until liquid is absorbed. Add all other ingredients (except raisins, nuts, sesame seeds and 2 tablespoons of flour) with eggs slightly beaten. Add the raisins and nuts at the end. Mix raisins with 2 tablespoons of flour so that they don't sink to the bottom of the pan. Mix with a wooden spoon. If the dough is too thick, add 2-4 tablespoons of milk. Pour into a 12-inch round pan. Sprinkle the top with sesame seeds. Bake in a 350° oven for one hour or until a knife inserted in center comes out clean.

DESSERTS & BREADS

TZALETIA

The following is the basic recipe.

1 cup corn flour

2 tablespoons sugar

4 tablespoons raisins

Peel and juice of half an orange

Oil for frying

Mix the ingredients together to form a thick dough. Spoon the mixture into hot oil and fry. Sprinkle with sugar and cinnamon or cover with honey.

Tzaletia are crisp, crunchy and a little bit on the heavy side for some people. To lighten them, I have used yeast and combined corn meal with flour. I deep-fry them as Loukoumades.

TZALETIA II

2 1/2 cups flour

1 1/2 cups corn flour

1 package dry yeast

1 teaspoon sugar

1/2 cup raisins

Peel and juice of half an orange

Oil for frying

Tzaletia is a specialty on the island of Corfu.

Dissolve yeast and sugar in lukewarm water. Add 1 1/2 cups of flour. Let it rise, doubling in

size. Add the remaining ingredients and mix well. Drop the dough by the tablespoonful into hot oil and deep fry. Cover with honey or sugar and cinnamon. Serve hot.

FRIED YAMS

In the winter, after my family had harvested the garden potatoes and yams, we would make a fried yam dessert.

Boil the yams until soft but firm. Cool and peel. Slice them into half-inch rounds. Fry them in oil until golden brown. Serve hot with sugar and cinnamon. Sometimes we dipped the yams into a batter of flour and water before frying them. Try them either way. They are delicious.

Greek Coffee

Greeks are very particular about their coffee and very precise in the way they order it.

Depending on the sweetness you want, you can have straight coffee without sugar (sketos); medium sweet (metrios); sweet (glykos) and very sweet (poli glykos).

You can have coffee with or without foam (kaimaki). Depending on the amount of coffee you use, you can have a light coffee (elafros) or a heavy one (varis). Making coffee is an art that is learned from mother to daughter and is transmitted through the generations.

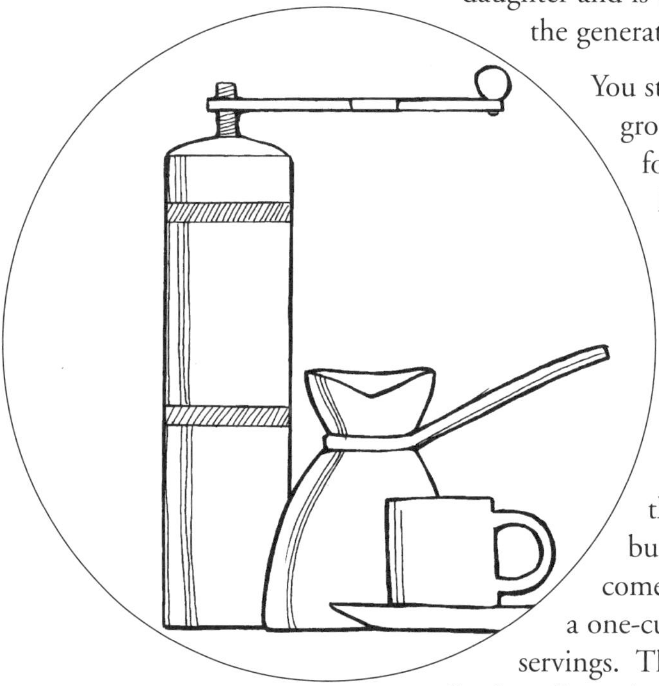

You start with a finely-ground coffee (not instant) found in Greek and Middle Eastern groceries. You will need a special coffeepot called briki. The pot is wide at the bottom and narrow at the neck, which widens to an open rim to allow the coffee foam to rise but not spill. Coffeepots come in different sizes, from a one-cup serving to several servings. The briki has a long handle that allows the cook to hold it without burning herself. Coffee is served in a demitasse. The cups are small and dainty, white or with elaborate designs. You never use cream with Greek coffee, and you serve it without a spoon.

When I go home, at the airport, they serve coffee in styrofoam cups. I find it too commercial. I think they are missing a characteristic of the Greek culture that is so unique.

For one cup, measure one demitasse of water, and pour in the briki. Put in the amount of sugar according to your taste and stir. Add one full teaspoon of coffee. Bring the water to a boil and watch it carefully. The coffee slowly mixes with the water and makes a foam. The foam rises very quickly, making a fizzing sound. Mother always said the coffee "sings to you." When it hits the high note, you need to remove it from the heat. Stir it with a spoon for the foam to come down (don't over-stir; you will have less foam). Repeat the process once or twice. Now the coffee is ready. Spoon some of the foam in each cup if preparing more than one. Fill the cups with the rest of the coffee. Serve with a glass of water.

Some people grind the coffee beans with a special grinder found in the same stores.

As this is not filtered, there is a sediment left in the cup, which you don't drink. You drink as much as possible down to the sediment.

Part of the ceremony of coffee-drinking is turning the cup with the sediment upside down to drain. This is done mostly among women. The sediment leaves a pattern that is interpreted by a fortune teller.

I drink to your good fortune!

MENUS

My friends asked me to include some menus that they can easily follow. Here are some extremely popular combinations in many Greek regions.

Fried dried cod
Garlic sauce (Skordalia)
Green beans or beets
This combination is frequently used during Lent.

Many Greek dishes are one-plate ones such as soups, vegetables Yiahni, accompanied by feta cheese, olives, smoked herring and fresh bread to dip in oil.

A menu that I frequently use while entertaining my friends in the United States is as follows:
Egg-lemon soup
Moussaka
Easy green beans and tomatoes
Greek salad and feta cheese
Cracked wheat pilaf with onions
Galatoboureko
Greek coffee
I have tried to change this menu numerous times but my guests insist on having moussaka over other selections. I have cooked moussaka hundreds of times and I don't need a recipe any more. I feel that I have moussaka power. As a matter of fact, I have a deep purple t-shirt that says, "MOUSSAKA POWER."

Macaroni or spaghetti is very popular on my island, followed by a meat dish like pastitsada, stifado, or kapama. Use the sauce of the meat dish to mix with the pasta and top it with grated Parmesan or other Greek hard cheeses. Mashed potatoes and a vegetable of your choice can accompany the meat.

Desserts are not always a part of a Greek menu. Desserts are used on special occasions like name days, celebrations, feasts, or tea parties. For a delicious pastry, you go to the local pastry shop.

We don't celebrate birthdays as much as name days. Most Greeks have a name associated with a saint of the Orthodox Church that has a special assigned day for celebration.

INDEX

E

F

G

H

I

K

L

M

N

O

P

Q

TO ORDER MORE COPIES OF

Corfu Cooking

by

Alice Padova Anderson

Send the form below to:

Athena Publishing Company
P.O. Box 584
Columbia, MO 65205

with **$24.95** for each copy
In Missouri add $1.80 sales tax for each copy
and $4.00 for each copy for shipping and handling.
(Sorry, no credit cards.)

NAME ____

ADDRESS ____

____

____

____

TO ORDER MORE COPIES OF

Corfu Cooking

by

Alice Padova Anderson

Send the form below to:

Athena Publishing Company
P.O. Box 584
Columbia, MO 65205

with **$24.95** for each copy
In Missouri add $1.80 sales tax for each copy
and $4.00 for each copy for shipping and handling.
(Sorry, no credit cards.)

NAME ____

ADDRESS ______________________________________

____

____

____